Muses

www.pocketessentials.com

Muses

JULIA FORSTER

POCKET ESSENTIALS

This edition published in 2007 by Pocket Essentials
P.O. Box 394, Harpenden, Herts, AL5 1XJ
www.pocketessentials.com

ISBN 10: 1-904048-71-4
ISBN 13: 978-1-904048-71-8

2 4 6 8 10 9 7 5 3 1

Typeset by Avocet Typeset, Chilton, Aylesbury, Bucks
Printed and bound in Great Britain by J.H. Haynes & Sons, Sparkford

For Heather Forster and Doreen Fletcher

In memoriam

Acknowledgements

To those who gave me the inspiration and provided the means to write this book, thank you: Ali Warner (for the house to research it in); Tom Crompton (for the house to write it in and for being there); Shirley Stewart (for the desk to write it on); Ion Mills and all at Oldcastle Books (for publishing it); Lindsay Clarke and Francis Gilbert (for the mentoring); Sara Allan and Theodore Zeldin (for the interviews) and Sam Duby and Katherine Symonds (for being constructively critical).

And for ongoing and unfailing support for this project and over the years, thanks to: Nicola Barr, Retta Bowen, Russell Celyn-Jones, Philip Cowell, the Gritti family, Cate Hall, David Morley, Nicola Perry, Roz and Roy at the Review bookshop in Peckham and everyone at The Hub London. Thanks finally to John Forster and Ken Forster, and to John and Sue Merriman.

'I want to remain on the untransmuted, untransformed, untransposed plane. This alchemy called creation, or fiction, has become for me as dangerous as the machine.'

— Anaïs Nin

'So I'm lying around and this thing comes as a whole piece, you know, words and music, and I think well, you know, can I say I wrote it? I don't know who the hell wrote it.'

— John Lennon

'If you sit down, unimpassioned and uninspired, and *tell* yourself to write for so many hours, you will merely produce... some of that article which fills, so far as I can judge, two-thirds of most magazines — most easy to write, most weary to read — men call it "padding", and it is, to my mind, one of the most detestable things in modern literature.'

— Lewis Carroll

Contents

CONTENTS

Introduction

Muses and Inspiration: Unexpected Gifts from Above?

The French novelist Gustave Flaubert mistrusted it, the philosopher Arthur Schopenhauer would argue in the middle of the street with the spirit that impelled it, and the composer Tchaikovsky reckoned that it only came to those able to master their disinclination. Inspiration is a slippery thing. The writer Gerard Manley Hopkins described it as 'a mood of great, abnormal in fact, mental acuteness, either energetic or receptive'[1] whereas the British comic genius John Cleese is quoted to have said, when asked where he got his ideas from, that 'A little man in Swindon gives them to me – but I don't know where he gets them from!'[2] Inspiration can motivate people to carry out feats of imaginative brilliance, to invent entirely new ways of perceiving the world and to create breathtaking works of art, literature or music. And, in the realm of inspiration, one thing is certain – muses have a large role to play.

Since the time of the ancient Greeks, when they first came into being, what a muse means has never been agreed upon. Writers and thinkers from that era disagreed even then on their provenance, their number, their names and which gods brought them into being. Attempts to portray and define the muse in recent history have been carried out by both intellectuals and Hollywood scriptwriters alike. In 1999, the movie *The Muse* was released in which Sharon Stone plays Sarah Little, the fickle and mentally unstable muse who claims to be able to inspire screenwriters from La La Land so long as she is put up in a penthouse with 24-hour room service. Earlier in the century the poet and intellectual Robert Graves wrote a tome on the muse called *The White Goddess* in which he wrote forthrightly that a woman who concerns herself with poetry should 'either be a silent Muse and inspire the poets by her womanly presence... or she should be the Muse in a complete sense... She should be the visible moon: impartial, loving, severe, wise.'[3]

More often than not, the prevailing notion of muses is that they are women. Usually they are beautiful, commonly they are mute and impossibly, and perhaps unselfconsciously, graceful. Just by virtue of her presence, as Graves writes, this traditional type of muse should inspire and intoxicate; she doesn't actually have to do anything but be. The archetype of the passive muse found in Ancient Greece and the Middle Ages has been shed in the centuries since then; muses have found their voice, and minds have opened to accommodate spiritual, male and mutual muses. This little book goes some way towards cataloguing a selection of those more traditional muses and then explodes the archetypal muse myth by looking at those spirited men, women and children of more recent times whose inspiration has proved indispensable.

Take Mae West as an example of the more modern muse: an outspoken siren of the silver screen from the golden age of Hollywood, famed for saying, 'Is that a gun in your pocket, or are you just glad to see me?' The cover to this book shows a replica of the surrealist artist Salvador Dalí's homage to the vampish actress: his red lip sofa inspired by Mae West's pout.[4] Made from satin and wood and created in 1938, the sofa was not the only act of immortalising the actress's fine features that Salvador Dalí attempted. He was fascinated by her face and, in another installation, superimposed an enlarged photo of it onto a room in a piece of art called 'Face of Mae West Which May Be Used as an Apartment.'

When feisty muses and artists get together it can become combustible – like sodium making contact with water. The first time that the poet Sylvia Plath meets her soul mate Ted Hughes she takes a bite of his cheek; when Salvador Dalí prepares to meet his future muse and wife, he shaves his armpits until they bleed and anoints himself with goat manure; but, perhaps the most volatile of all, William S. Burroughs accidentally shoots his drugged-up muse point blank in the head: far from the ideal of muse as a mute maiden.

For the German writer and philosopher Johann Wolfgang von Goethe, when the highest kind of inspiration strikes, he described it as being an 'unexpected gift from above', not of man's own making but given by the gods. Yet it seems that certain people are particularly gifted at fostering and fuelling startling creative works within an artist's psyche. More specifically, it is the relationship between a muse and an artist which has the potential to ignite in the artist something akin to divine inspiration – a watershed moment, a brilliant insight, a radical expression. By first learning about these alliances between muse and artist, and then by exploring what the critical factor in the muse relationship was for the artist, we can begin to reveal the nature of inspiration itself. This is inspiration in the context of human relationships and, in many instances, in the context of a love which bonds the artist and muse together – sometimes across continents, often beyond words and, occasionally, in spite of each other.

If inspiration is the pot at the end of the rainbow, the final two chapters are an attempt to get even closer to it. By meeting and interviewing a contemporary philosopher, novelist and artist, the role inspiration is playing in the twenty-first century is scrutinised and, to finish the book off with a bang, we ask what is it out there in the ether or deep within each of us which allows amazing outputs of creativity. The ideas in this final chapter are viewed from the standpoint of some of the recent discoveries in the world of quantum science which favour a holistic and participatory view of the nature of everything; because, if there is just one thing in common between all the muses and artists examined in this book, it is that they are in a relationship, and a very meaningful relationship, with each other.

One last word about the case studies presented in the following chapters. This Pocket Essential catalogues just a few of the men and women throughout the ages without whom some of the greatest works of art, literature and music would never have been created. Would that it could also catalogue those muses who have catalysed some of the most amazing scientific discoveries, acts of bravery or sporting achievements but there was not enough space. So, for the sake of consistency, I've stuck to the arts and, rather than approach musedom in a linear fashion, in most instances I've grouped together two or more muses (not necessarily from the same historical period) in order to complement and contrast the muses' relationships with and influence on their artists.

The Roots of Musedom

Pausanias, Hesiod, The White Goddess, Plato, Neo-Platonists and Gnosticism

According to accounts by Pausanias, the peripatetic Greek geographer and historian of the second century AD, there were originally three mountain goddess muses. Pausanias's *Descriptions of Greece* were like early Baedeker guides and it is in the ninth of his ten books that we learn about the three muses: 'They say that Ephialtes and Otos were the first men to sacrifice to the Muses on [Mount] Helikon and to declare this mountain sacred to the Muses'.[5] Pausanias goes on to say that, according to the writer Hegesinous (who pre-dated Pausanias), a dwelling called Askre was founded at the foot of Mount Helicon by the sons of Aloeus and by Oioklos, who was parented by Askre and Poseidon. The sons of Aloeus believed that there were three muses called Melete (study or practice), Mneme (memory) and Aoide (song). The more common recollection of the muses from this era is that there were nine of them, and Pausanias explains that Pieros of Macedon established and named them at Thespiai. This number nine is echoed in the

Theogony, by Hesiod who lived even earlier than Pausanias, around 700 BC, and within sight of Mount Helicon in Boeotia.

Hesiod worked as a shepherd on his father's land and maintained that it was while he was out in the fields one day, tending his lambs, that he was visited by the muses, given a sceptre of laurel and instructed to become a poet. To invoke the muses at the beginning of any artistic endeavour quickly became a tradition and one which lasted for many centuries. And so Hesiod's long poem, the *Theogony*, commences with a conventional hymn in honour of the muses which lasts a total of 104 lines and begins, 'From the Muses of Helicon, let us begin our singing, that haunt Helicon's great and holy mountain, and dance on their soft feet round the violet-dark spring and the altar of the mighty son of Kronos'.[6] Hesiod's account sees the muses' parentage as being that of Memory, who was Queen of the foothill of Eleutherae, and of the son of the god Kronos. He writes that the muses were of one mind, blessed with beautiful singing voices, and that they would sing, celebrate and dance on and around the holy Mount Helicon. Hesiod adds that they were also blessed with the kind of characteristics below, which perhaps begins to explain why the muses always have been – and still are – such slippery beings. In describing themselves, the muses say:

> we know to tell many lies that sound like truth,
> but we know to sing reality when we will.[7]

In later accounts, the nine muses were believed to influence their own individual realm of arts, humanities or science. These realms varied, depending on the fashions of various times, but the muses always kept a close allegiance with the humanities and sciences, and with education and creativity. The most commonly reported alignments of muse and realm are:

Muse	Realm
Calliope	Epic poetry
Clio	History
Erato	Erotic poetry
Euterpe	Music and lyric poetry
Melpomene	Tragedy
Polyhymnia	Sacred lyrics, rhetoric, geometry
Terpsichore	Dance
Thalia	Comedy and bucolic poetry
Urania	Astronomy and astrology

These later muses, all of them female goddesses, were the offspring of the god Zeus and the goddess Mnemosyne, a name which translates as 'memory' and which has its roots in the word for 'moon'. This fecund goddess was daughter to the great goddess Gaia (Earth) and the god Ouranos (Heaven) and, for those that worshipped the muses, it was (and still is) seen as of great significance that the muses were from such a primal, earthly parentage. When the inspiration of the muses was invoked by Greek artists, poets or philosophers they would, in effect, be calling upon both the world's memory and their capacity to use their imagination to inform their work or composition. Memory catalysed the arts and sciences in the Hellenic world, and the Greeks took the muses and their parents very seriously. Pythagoras, who founded the first philosophical school, dedicated it to the muses. For the Greeks, the muses were a useful means to catalogue artistic endeavours and scientific experience – but more than that they were sacred and, as such, remained elusive; the muses possessed organic and almost orgiastic qualities.

Since those times, muse worship has gone through many transformations and reformations. Some of the most informative and recent retellings of muse and moon goddess worship are found in Robert Graves' *The White Goddess* and in the works of Joseph Campbell, for example in his *Primitive Mythology* volumes. Both writers explain the way in which societies have shifted from worshipping feminine, Gaian and matriarchal icons to patriarchal worship centred on masculine, fatherly qualities. This shift coincides with the way in which the culture of cities overrode agrarian cultures. Those cultures which partook in moon-worship did so, Graves argues, because they recognised a natural affinity between the female and planet earth, its seasons and the influence of the moon on the female's menstrual cycle. The feminine was sacred, powerful and terrifying.

So far, the muses seem at best ambiguous and at worst unreliable. These wise icons embody inspiration, give pleasure and insight, have memories that reach back as long as the planet has existed and have the capacity to intoxicate, excite and arouse those that invoke them. In Graves' words, to invoke a muse gives the 'experience of mixed exaltation and horror that her presence excites'[8] and, if this invocation is done truly by a poet, the resulting poem should send shivers down the reader's spine, make his eyes water and his hairs stand on end. The power imbued by the energy from the 'Mother of All Living' found in the true poem has its roots in forces so ancient that the true poet falls in love and breaks his heart longing for her.

Plato, the thinker, writer and mathematician who was alive and philosophising from c.427 – c.347 BC, created his own intellectual temple to the muses in the grove Academus, where he held his seminars. Plato's philosophical writings took the form of dialogues: conversations between his trusty literary mouthpiece, Socrates, the older philosopher to whom the younger and more impressionable Plato had once listened, and an unsuspecting second participant in the discussions who often provided the counterpoint to Socrates. These secondary characters were sometimes based on real people from the era and, by playing on their curiosity or the fuzzy logic they demonstrated, Plato was able, through the dialogues, to postulate his own theories on a miscellany of ideas about such topics as love, ethics, the ideal state and the nature of inspiration. In Plato's dialogues, just as in real life, Socrates is seen wandering barefoot around the city of Athens, writing nothing down, only occasionally scraping the odd stick along the ground to demonstrate a geometric principle.

In one of Plato's more mature dialogues, the *Phaedrus,* Socrates suggests that he and Phaedrus should sit on a grassy knoll by a meandering stream within earshot of the melodic cicadas to continue their discourse. Socrates's opinion is that the true lover of the muses is not the poet but the philosopher and he outlines the four different types of divine madness. In Socrates's schema, the third type of possession is by none other than the muses. According to Socrates, when the inspiration of the muses takes hold of the 'gentle and virgin soul', it rouses him to write and express himself through verse. In a lovely passage which should warm the cockles of all crazed bards out there, Socrates says that the lunatic poet will always out-write the conscientious versifier:

> ...if a man comes to the door of poetry untouched by the madness of the Muses, believing that technique alone will make him a good poet, he and his sane compositions never reach perfection, but are utterly eclipsed by the perform-ances of the inspired madman.[9]

The different realms of the muses are fleshed out in this dialogue and a hierarchy of musedom is developed which sees the muses of philosophy, of course, at the number one spot.

This heaven-sent madness is also referenced in another of Plato's dialogues, the *Ion*, in which Socrates says that, unless the poet is out of his senses and his mind, he will not create new work for 'not by art does the poet sing, but by power divine'.[10] Here Socrates elucidates the effect that such muse-impelled poetry can have on an audience and says that the muse has an energy like a magnet. First, the muse inspires the poet who drops all reason for the intoxicating state of inspiration and, in turn, the poet draws his audience with this poetic power. Socrates makes the distinction clear between art and emotion and relegates poetry to the emotional in this dialogue, as it is not governed by rules and rationale but by inspiration.

Elsewhere in the Platonic philosophy we learn that the muses and their heritage have other roles to play in human nature; in the *Thaetetus* Socrates explains that in each individual's soul there can be found a block of wax which varies in quality depending on the person and is a gift to each soul from Mnemosyne. His ideas may seem a little outmoded to the modern-day anatomist, but Socrates believed that whenever we see something, hear a sound or think a thought it becomes imprinted in the wax. The mother of the muses – Memory – is, in some ways, the root of all knowledge for both Socrates and Plato, for both believed that we already know everything there is to know from the moment we are born and that education – which the muses presided over – was our way of remembering everything our eternal souls have forgotten. No wonder that the word 'museum' is derived from the same root as muse: the place where everything ancient is kept lest we forget it.

In the fourteenth and fifteenth centuries, Platonic texts enjoyed a rediscovery and rebirth by way of the Neo-

Platonists. This was an era that, with its re-claiming of learning and civilised behaviour, would partly come to define European culture as it is today. Many see this period as being one in which the psychology of the individual burgeoned and, in a rich climate of experimentation, especially in the development of humanist thought, writers and thinkers began to place man within a wider scheme of things. This was the century, after all, that witnessed Columbus sail the ocean blue and discover America: the world was suddenly becoming bigger. And so the Florentine Marsilio Ficino (1433–99) was born into a period that honoured remembrance of classical texts and the radicalisation of religious beliefs. His birth, just 100 years after the Black Death had struck, was crucial in re-establishing the Platonic canon.

Ficino was invited to take the role of head of the Platonic Academy in Careggi in 1463 and, from his scholarly seat there, he espoused the Platonic philosophy. His sixteenth-century biographer, Giovanni Corsi, paints an interesting picture of this golden-haired Neo-Platonist: a vegetarian and a stammerer, Ficino would regularly rise with the sun, if not a couple of hours before, and possessed scant material goods, yet he had a love of excellent wine. Ficino, Corsi writes 'was not at all inclined to sensual passion, but he was rapt in love... and used to converse and debate with the young about love in the Socratic manner'.[11] Although Ficino developed his own philosophy on the nature of inspiration for which he coined the phrase *'divino furore'* or 'divine frenzy', one which was much indebted to Plato's dialogues on the muses and the holy insanity that they inspired, he stayed chaste throughout his life. Yet, in the eyes of his contemporaries and patrons, Ficino had divine frenzy aplenty. He was an accomplished musician as well as being an intellectual, doctor and, by 1473, a priest. After he played his Orphic lyre one time to the Bishop Campano, the Bishop wrote of his performance that it was 'as if curly-headed Apollo took up the lyre of Marsilio and fell victim to his own song. Frenzy arises, His eyes catch fire... and he discovers music which he never learnt.'[12]

It is in his 'Seventh Letter', written on 1 December 1457 to Peregrino Agli,[13] that Ficino revisits the muses' inspired madness that Plato had written about centuries before. In this letter, which is a fascinating complement to Plato's *Phaedrus*, he writes a brief précis of Plato's definition of the four types of madness and of how it is that men can only remember the divine if they are stirred by their senses to recollect it by its shadows or images through the bodily senses:

> But we do indeed perceive the reflection of divine beauty with our eyes and mark the resonance of divine harmony with our ears those bodily senses which Plato considers the most perceptive of all. Thus when the soul has received through the physical senses those images which are within material objects, we remember what we knew before when we existed outside the prison of the body.

When the soul recollects this memory – notice the role of memory here – it shakes its wings and gradually distances itself from the filthy body and becomes 'wholly possessed by divine frenzy'.

In Ficino's understanding, recollection of the divine comes through two bodily sensors: the eyes and the ears. By hearing divine harmonies, such as the sound of the planets and the heavens in orbit which produce a marvellous concordance, souls are again reminded of their pre-bodily existence when they were in the realm of the eternal (it's important to note that Platonic thought argues that our souls are eternal). On hearing the divine music, the soul returns to an ancient memory of harmonic bliss and flaps its wings in a bid to return to this source of the divine sound. On the earthly plane, when mortal musicians imitate the heavenly form of music inspired by the muses they will perform the kind of song which, like the poetry lauded by Robert Graves, sends shivers down the spine. Ficino's gloss on Plato's muse-inspired song is that it therefore follows that 'poetry springs from divine frenzy, frenzy from the Muses, and the Muses from Jove'. The influence of Jove on the muses is accredited by Ficino's predecessors, the Platonists and by the followers of Pythagoras who believed that Jove represented and nourished the complete universe and everything within it.

An interesting spin-off from the Neo-Platonist conception of inspiration which would flourish in the Baroque era is that of the Gnostics. For those who followed Gnosticism, it was the individual who held the spark of divine knowledge and this tradition of thought took its inspiration from a blend of religious belief systems including Judaism and

Christianity, as well as the Neo-Platonic system. Echoing Plato's view that the world is an inferior replica of the divine, the Gnostics believed that we live in an ignorant constellation of planets created by anti-spiritual rulers and dictated by fate or destiny. In this second-rate cosmos, divine sparks are bound by their material constraints and these sparks aspire towards returning to their former spiritual existence. Salvation is found in a spiritual type of self-knowledge and it is the duty of the heavenly redeemers to descend from the Pleromatic Source to bring Gnosis – the esoteric knowledge of spiritual truths which are cloaked on the physical plane.

Opinions on why the Gnostic cult developed have varied, mainly because it sat on the edges of several religious traditions, but it was certainly viewed by most at the time to be a heretical and radical tradition and one which, flying in the face of orthodox religious beliefs, instead took a nihilistic outlook on the world and its values. Its legitimisation of people's experience of inspiration in the pursuit of wisdom put knowledge back in the hands of the individual and democratised divinity; divine knowledge was no longer sourced from sacred texts or from abstract gods, but from each human being's sacred experience of rekindling the divine spark within himself or herself. Although ancient, the Gnostic approach to inspiration is perhaps most fitting to transplant into the western democratic world with its tendency towards privileging the individual. Inspiration, for both the Gnostics and for the modern artist, moves from the realm of the gods to the realm of reality.

Archetypal Muses

The Troubadour Tradition: Courtly Love

No examination of the nature of inspiration and musedom would be complete without a dip into the history of just a few of the most important and archetypal muses. Different centuries and countries have spawned new traditions of identifying with the female of the species. Most notably, the troubadours from the Provençal region of France – then known as Occitania – created the tradition of 'courtly love' which has been critical in shaping Western attitudes to what we still refer to as 'courtship' today.

The first known troubadour is Guilhem VII Count of Poitou, IX Duke of Aquitaine (1071–1127) who practised in the court of Poitiers. As a troubadour, the Duke of Aquitaine was an entertainer, poet and wordsmith all at once. Between the years of 1100 and 1300 in French and European courts, it was the troubadour's role to write original lyrics and devise accompanying music which they would then perform for the pleasure of the courtly men and women – the troubadour's craft was an early and westernised version of inspired writing. 'Troubadour' comes from the word '*trobar*', the Provençal equivalent of the Latin word '*invenire*' which meant 'to discover' or 'to invent', and this romantic tradition bore new styles of rhetoric and versification – the '*canso*', for example, was a favourite mode of versifying. Troubadours came from regions beyond Provence, as far east as the Alps and as far west as the Auvergne. They travelled widely and their songs were richly textured by their experiences of visiting European courts where they would be influenced by sights, sounds and foreign musical composition.

Over 2,500 original troubadour songs still survive and the history books contain names of 460 troubadours whose work would go on to inform and inspire European poetry for centuries.[14] The world of the troubadour was just as politicised as ours and their medium allowed them the opportunity to comment on the concerns of the day through song. Although this tradition of inspired writing was relatively short-lived, it was structured, highly stylised and subject to the conventions that the form demanded. Ironically, this feudal era which would idolise women through poetry and place them on a pedestal was also highly misogynistic and patriarchal.

In true feminist fashion, however, there was a backlash by the women of the age. Although the trobaritz tradition of female troubadours has not been as well documented as that of their male counterparts, it is known that a small troupe of them existed in the south of France, writing between 1150 and 1250. These female bards were mostly privileged noblewomen, and had probably already been subjected to idolisation by the troubadours through their poetry. Some academics believe that this was one of the earliest forms of feminism: women standing up for their right to have a voice. 'To all the valiant women/who have sung and gone unsung,'[15] reads one of the scarce verses from the trobaritz songs. Only 30 or so exist – it's difficult to know exactly how many because few are accredited to their female authors. The content of their works is similar to that of the troubadour tradition and they focus on '*fin'amor*' which translates as the idea of true, pure love. Even in an era much renowned for its fetishisation of the feminine form, it would appear that sisters were already doing it for themselves, and finding their own mouthpiece for the inspiration of true love.

Dante and Beatrice: Glorious Lady of my Mind

Throughout Europe during the Middle Ages the nine classical muses were a widespread image found throughout literature, in al fresco paintings, mosaics and even in the tarot cards. But one of the most famous medieval muses was Dante's Beatrice. Born in 1264 in Florence, Italy, Dante Alighieri completed his lyric poem *La Vita Nuova* (*The New Life*) before he turned 30. He was inspired to compose this autobiographical writing by two sightings of his muse, Beatrice, a muse in the untouchable tradition who is now mostly accepted to have been Beatrice Portinari (c.1265–1290). Dante saw her once when they were both in their ninth year and again nine years later.

From the time that Dante first set eyes on Beatrice, his unrequited love for her governed his soul – so it is perhaps fitting that the name Beatrice means 'she who brings blessedness'. On seeing her, he writes in the opening pages of *La Vita Nuova* that she is a stronger deity than he is, and that she will govern him. Wonder-struck, Dante realises that from that moment his soul will be eternally disturbed by having known her.

La Vita Nuova is an account of Dante's intense passion for this muse-beauty. There are scant accounts of meetings between Dante and Beatrice but it is known that, by the time of their second encounter when they were about 18, Beatrice was married to Simone de'Bardi, and Dante betrothed to Gemma Donati, whom he would go on to marry and have seven children by. In the archetypal muse tradition, however, this insurmountable hurdle between them did not inhibit Dante's imagination or his ability to draw from this purely platonic and imaginative bond. The contemporary Scottish poet Don Paterson offers an insight into this type of muse-artist relationship: 'If she's real, and especially if she's dead,' Paterson writes, the relationship 'should remain unconsummated, because that infinite delay and anticipation is precisely what provides the ache, the wound, that hollow feeling that only art can fill… temporarily, of course'.[16] And Beatrice would die young, still in her twenties and untouched by Dante, in the year 1290.

Although *La Vita Nuova* is seminal in the history of 'love literature', at the time of composition, Dante felt that his sonnets written in Beatrice's honour did not scale the same heights as the pedestal upon which he had placed her. It would not be until Dante finished, just before his death, *La Divina Commedia* (*The Divine Comedy*) that he found a role that truly honoured his Beatrice. In this love poem, Dante writes about the soul's journey from Hell or Inferno to Purgatory and then to Paradise. Beatrice instructs Virgil to rescue Dante from the dark wood of Inferno and from Mount Purgatory onwards, Dante is placed in the hallowed hands of Beatrice to complete the ascent to the Earthly Paradise. Dante confesses to Beatrice that he loved another after her death but Beatrice smiles lovingly at him, a smile with the power to transport him through the heavens while she assumes her place in the Rose of the Blessed in the Empyrean.

Literary commentators use Beatrice as an example of a muse turned into an allegory, for, in *La Divina Commedia,* she comes to symbolise more abstract qualities such as grace or redemption. Whichever reading is bestowed upon Beatrice, one fact remains: Dante's relationship with her is certainly the most resonant example of the idealised, unconsummated and mute muse in literary history. It is a troubling fact of musedom that, like Dante's soul, the artist's can be shaken to the core simply by having glimpsed their source of inspiration. These muses may incite a white heat of creativity for years to follow, but as many artists come to discover, this afflatus comes at a cost.

Petrarch and Laura: The World's Delight is but a Brief Dream

If Beatrice were to have any competition for the number one spot of fourteenth-century Italian muses, it would surely be Laura, muse to the poet and humanist Francesco Petrarch (1304–1374). Who Petrarch's Laura was in real life is uncertain and some doubt her very existence, but when she is identified, it is most commonly as Laure de Noves, who was born six years before Petrarch in 1310 and who died at the hands of either the Black Death or a pulmonary complication linked to having given birth to no fewer than 11 children. Like Beatrice, Laura was unobtainable: when Francesco first saw her in 1327, she had been married for two years to Hugo de Sade. And, if it was indeed this Laura with whom Petrarch became besotted, then her descendants would include the infamous Marquis de Sade.

His first glimpse of Laura was on Good Friday 1327 which fell on 6 April – the very same day on which Laura died in 1348 at the age of 38. At the time, they were both attending a service at the church of Sainte Claire d'Avignon. It was unrequited, impossible and unendurable love at first sight. Don Paterson again: 'We usually don't hear from [the muse]... because we've conveniently banged her up in heaven somewhere, or – if she's not dead or made up – because her social milieu tends, conveniently, not to intersect with that of the poets.'[17] Indeed, according to Dante's secret book, the *Secretum*, Laura was to refuse to interact with Petrarch because convention would not allow it: she was betrothed to another.

Despite his unrequited love and, indeed, by virtue of it, Petrarch enjoyed a rich career as a poet: his version of the sonnet (the versification still referred to today as the 'Petrarchan sonnet') won him many accolades and the title of Poet Laureate in 1341. The poems addressed to Laura in *Canzoniere* (*Song Book*) were among his most highly regarded. Petrarch's Laura became a celebrity of her age, the pinnacle of the ideal woman. Petrarch would pen over 300 love lyrics in praise of her and, although he would remain an unmarried scholar, he fathered two illegitimate children (neither to Laura).

Laura is the ultimate muse as *tabula rasa* or blank canvas, a role which each muse in this book plays, some to a greater extent than others. But the puritanical pedestal on which these archetypal muses stood will be wobbled by more contemporary muses. Compared to the ideal muse-woman of the Middle Ages, more recent muses drive their artists to the edges, where things get a bit more gritty, and can involve incest, imprisonment and institutionalisation. This tension is still apparent in the archetypal muses, though it is, perhaps, less taut. After all, what would have happened to all that pent-up poetic energy, ripe to be projected onto the unassuming muse, had Petrarch married Laura or Dante kissed his Beatrice?

Beloved Muses: William Butler and George Yeats; John Keats and Fanny Brawne

William Butler and George Yeats: The Wisdom of Two

The most noteworthy chapter in the marriage between William Butler Yeats and his wife, Bertha George Yeats, demands a little suspension of disbelief. An eight-and-a-half-year-long creative collaboration between the couple resulted in the book *A Vision: An Explanation of Life,* which purports to explain 'The Way of the Soul between the Sun and the Moon' and was written automatically by Yeats's wife, inspired by séances and sittings, somnambulant journeys, dream-speaking and deep meditations. Born out of these spiritual encounters was a philosophical system, inspired by some other-worldly energy, which threw light on the psychology of the individual, the mathematical law of history, the adventure of the soul after death and the interaction between the living and the dead.

The final version of *A Vision* was published on 15 January 1926 under WB Yeats's name. In fact the book was jointly authored, a fact which George (or Georgie) Yeats did not want made public, but which William felt was crucial to its very existence. Four days after their marriage on 20 October 1917 – in William's fifty-third year, one which had seen him propose no fewer than three times to three different women – George and William began their voyage into the unconscious from the privacy of their honeymoon suite in Ashdown Forest Hotel. George plumbed the depths of their matrimonial union at a psychic level, unearthing Yeats's innate creativity through the writings which were 'given' to her to write down in front of his eyes. Yeats had a long acquaintance with the spiritual domain; he had attended his first séance in 1886, became a member of the Order of the Golden Dawn in 1890 and frequently turned to the spirits for inspiration for his poetry. He wrote of this psychic watershed with George: 'What came in disjointed sentences, in almost illegible writing, was so exciting, sometimes so profound, that I persuaded her to give an hour or two day after day to the unknown writer, and after some half-dozen such hours offered to spend what remained of life explaining and piecing together those scattered sentences.'[18] But the spirits did not offer any explanation, merely dictating through George that they had come to give William metaphors for his poetry.

George and William first met in 1911 when George was the ripe age of 18, and William, aged 46, over 25 years her senior. By this time, William was already intimate with his 'spiritual opposite', a being called Leo Africanus with whom he would correspond in automatic writing. The day they first encountered each other, George had played truant from art school and taken herself to the British Museum and it was there that she caught her first glimpse of William Butler Yeats as he hurtled past her 'like a meteor'. That afternoon, she went for tea with her mother at the house of the writer Olivia Shakespear and was formally introduced to him; ironically, Olivia was one of Yeats's past lovers. Yeats's other big love was the Anglo-Irish beauty Maud Gonne, whom he'd met at the turn of the century and who, although fond of William, did not reciprocate his passionate feelings, turning him down when he proposed. Her beauty at least inspired him to write two plays for her, *The Countess Cathleen* and *Cathleen Ní Houlihan*, both of which became very successful.

After the marriage, George became the central muse and medium to William's *A Vision*; between 20 October 1917 and 28 March 1920, the couple committed to paper over 3,500 pages of notes and transcripts which took them more than 450 sittings. Each sitting was exclusive; the couple allowed nobody else to observe or witness the strange happenings which, as well as taking place in their hotel honeymoon suite, also followed them from their matrimonial home, Stone Cottage, to London and Oxford and to sojourns in Irish hotels from Dublin to Glendalough. The process of receiving messages from the spirit world involved complicated systems and dealings with spiritual 'personalities' who worked within clear hierarchies and demanded that the married couple use strictly defined techniques to log the incoming information.

Broadly speaking, George worked as a medium with

'Communicators' or 'Instructors' of whom there were three main ones called Thomas, Ameritus and Dionertes. There was also a (usually masculine) 'Control', accompanied by a helper, who would ensure that the communication George received passed the quality test, that the communication lasted the correct length of time and that it contained the right information. Names of the Control were sometimes anagrams, sometimes references to the ancient gods or poets of old. The Communicators' attempts to express what they had a burning desire to say could be impeded by 'Frustrators' when it became the role of the 'Guides,' called Leaf, Fish, Apple and Rose, to light up the way. Unlike so many other communicants with the spirit world, William and George did not try to summon up the voices of family, friends or famous people from the past, preferring to receive whatever important missive was due to them and then decode it together afterwards.

The demands placed upon George in undertaking this role of spiritual muse and medium were strenuous; being in the deep trance-like state tested her physical, emotional and psychic strength to the limits. She had to be an able receptor, capable of creating the conditions within herself to allow her to receive the messages. After committing the scrawled communications to paper, which she often had to write at great speed and which included not just odd juxtapositions of words but also symbols and numbers, she would then go through a process of deciphering the script with William, cataloguing the insights for *A Vision* which Yeats would latterly call his 'public philosophy'. This muse, who was remarkably perceptive and intuitive, would also share dreams with Yeats, and would continue to go into trances until a revised edition of *A Vision* was published for the second time in 1937 with a refined codification of the systematic thoughts.

The mores and social conduct of the time would not have looked kindly upon this kind of spiritual ventriloquism, which perhaps suggests why George was keen not to be known as a collaborator on the project. One can only guess why she put herself up for the role of dummy. Some biographers suggest that her original motive was to lift her newly-wed husband out of his melancholic moods and the guilt he was feeling for leaving Maud Gonne who, although she had rejected his proposals, remained the love of his life. Little did George know that she would unlock such a vast supernatural chest. And it was, ultimately, her mediumistic prowess that made *A Vision* possible, a fact of which the Instructors often reminded the couple. Only a woman of solid self-belief and vivid character could have sustained this role, survived its ambiguities and trusted the collaborative and creative process to such an impressive extent.

The wisdom of two people coming together can produce something outside of the ordinary. As Yeats said: 'No mind's contents are necessarily shut off from another and in moments of excitement images pass from one mind to the other with extraordinary ease, perhaps most easily from that portion of the mind which for the time being is outside consciousness... The second mind sees what the first has already seen – that is all.'[19] There is something particularly empowering and explosive about the inspirational power which George Yeats perfected during the period of collaborative writing with her husband. This is inspiration at its spiritual climax and at its most rarefied yet radical. Yeats's union with his wife demonstrates in bold terms how effectively the muse can act as a conduit to inspiration. Like the mythical journey of Eurydice, a muse's trajectory can transport her into an underworld which may be perilous but is rich with forbidden treasures, archetypal knowledge and shamanistic insights.

John Keats and Fanny Brawne: The Muse Next Door

'The roaring of the wind is my wife and the Stars through the window pane are my Children.'[20] Keats wrote this just a few days before meeting Fanny Brawne, the love – and muse – of his life. A young man with a rare poetic sensitivity, Keats found in elegant Fanny Brawne his ideal bride-never-to-be: tragically they never made it down the aisle, as Keats fell victim to tuberculosis three years after meeting Fanny.

Born five years after Keats in 1800, Fanny was the eldest of five children. The family was a distinguished one; some of Fanny's ancestors had been knighted and the family could trace its stock as far back as the Stuart period. The Brawnes lived in Hampstead, right by the Heath and, as an infant, Fanny formed a strong bond with the natural world. She grew up to become sensitive and sparky, loquacious and disarmingly opinionated, especially in the matters of fashion which she followed religiously, often drawing attention to her blue eyes by neatly accessorising her hair with beautiful blue ribbons.

Described by the poet Louis MacNeice as a 'sensuous mystic', Keats accomplished amazing poetic feats during his short life – he lived only to the age of 25. In the late eighteenth and early nineteenth centuries, illness and early death were, of course, common factors of everyday life and many of Keats' family met their deaths at an early age. His father, a stable keeper, had passed away when John was nine and his mother fell foul of tuberculosis six years later. His brother, Tom, was a victim of the same disease in 1818, the year in which Keats met his fiancée. At the time of their meeting, Keats was working on one of his greatest poems, *Endymion,* and he had retreated to Scotland just before its publication for a hiking tour with his friend Charles Armitage Brown. When Keats returned to London to be by the bedside of his dying brother, Tom, he moved into Charles Brown's house, Wentworth Place in Hampstead, half of which Charles had been renting out to the Brawne family while Keats was on holiday. Mrs Brawne, her son, Sam, and her two daughters, Fanny and Margaret, moved to nearby Elm Cottage on Charles Brown's return.

The go-between for the lovers' first meeting was the Dilke family, who lived in the other half of Wentworth Place and were mutual friends of both Keats and Fanny. Keats and Fanny would often see each other in the Dilke household but Keats was, at first, flummoxed by Fanny's coquettish nature. Consumed by the care of his dying brother and by worries about his own fragile health, he probably found it a valuable distraction to be in the company of this outspoken and elegant sixteen-year-old woman. He later wrote to his older brother, George, who had emigrated to America with his newly-wed wife Georgiana, that he found Fanny to be 'elegant, graceful, silly, fashionable and strange'.[21] Their courtship commenced in earnest in the autumn of 1818 and, that winter, Keats received and accepted an invitation to spend Christmas Day with the Brawne family at Elm Cottage. In return, Fanny received and accepted a proposal of marriage. However, it is doubtful if their early courtship was all plain-sailing. Fanny's mother, as a single parent, would have wanted a bright future for her daughter and Keats, on paper, was little more than a failed medical student with weak lungs (he had chosen writing over his medical career, which had been picked out for him). None the less, in April 1819, fate brought Fanny and Keats closer together when the Dilke family made the decision to move to inner city London and let their half of Wentworth Place to the Brawnes.

The proximity of this beguiling and, by all accounts very attractive, young woman was almost too much for the sensitive Keats to bear. During the spring, the couple got to know each other very well; Miss Brawne encouraging him to write, Mr Keats penning sonnets for the muse next door. 'Bright Star, would I were steadfast as thou art' is one of the many that he composed in honour of his disarming fiancée. Love provided him with a fresh inspiration which possessed him like an illness and his poetic voice became more refined, his style more self-assured but, again, this was not without its drawbacks. Keats found it impossible to think of Fanny 'without some sort of energy'[22] and this was energy that, in a poet's most regimented state of mind, should ideally be channelled into writing verse. Her distracting proximity didn't stop him from writing some of his greatest works that spring and early summer and, beneath the plum bush which lent a little shade to the lawn, Keats composed *Ode to a Nightingale* within weeks of Fanny's move to Wentworth Place. That fruitful period also saw him write *Eve of St. Agnes* and many other great odes including *Ode to a Grecian Urn* and *Ode to Psyche*.

Circumstances dictated that the amorous couple be separated as Brown let out Wentworth House for the summer of 1819. Keats and Fanny were forced to resort to an epistolary relationship, the poet writing from the Isle of Wight and then the cathedral city of Winchester in southern England. This period apart from his beloved saw Keats produce 1,500 lines of verse – not bad for someone whose health was in such continual decline that, by the time he returned to Hampstead in the late autumn, he was seriously concerned for his wellbeing. A letter Keats wrote to his fiancée in that October betrays the intensity of his feelings for her, and hints at the influence that Fanny had: 'My love has made me selfish. I cannot exist without you. I am forgetful of every thing but seeing you again – my Life seems to stop there – I see no further. You have absorb'd me.'[23]

Tragically, Keats' life was indeed grinding to a premature halt: he was being taken over by the onset of tuberculosis, the deadly illness characterised by coughing up blood and by severe weight loss. Keats' genetically weak immune system and, perhaps, his phlegmatic constitution, meant that he soon became a pale comparison of his former self both as poet and lover. His bride-to-be took on the role of nurse with aplomb, visiting daily and leaving Keats love letters on his sick bed. But, in the early part of 1820, Keats suffered a heart attack and the hard decision was made to ban Fanny from visiting, or even writing to her fiancé from next door for fear that the excitement would cause another attack.

On hearing of Keats' failing health, his friend and fellow poet Leigh Hunt invited Keats to spend some time at his home in Hampstead. The diversion helped but the thought of surviving another cold British winter did not. And so, in mid-September 1820, Keats accepted the invitation of fellow poet and friend Shelley to join him in Italy and set sail for the Mediterranean aboard the *Maria Crowther* in the knowledge that it would be warmer there – and that he would be far away from Fanny when he met the miserable death he knew was awaiting him. In his last letter to his lover, dated the month before he left for Italy, Keats wrote that the world was simply too brutal for him, and that he was glad that there was such a thing as a grave. Keats passed away the following year on 23 February in Rome. The epitaph chiselled on his gravestone reads: 'Here lies one whose name was writ in water.'

At the same time as Fanny was the object of his affection, and undoubtedly the energetic source of much of his inspiration, Keats was also developing his own theories about the imagination, inspiration and how best to prosper in poetical life. His theory of 'Negative Capability' contains, at its heart, a manifesto to live in the moment and in a state of being constantly non-judgemental. Keats describes Negative Capability as that capacity of man to remain 'in uncertainties, mysteries, doubts, without any irritable reaching after fact and reason'.[24] To complement the inspiration he found in Fanny Brawne, Keats had an unusually rare ability to let go of intellectual concerns and to mute what nowadays we might call the 'internal editor' which every writer fears: the little gremlin which sits atop the writer's shoulder and scrutinises every creative leap.

Most poets possess, to an extent, the ability to allow chance or magic to take its course but Keats was incredibly rare in his intuitiveness and his empathetic ability to energetically *become*, through his imagination, what he was describing in his verse. The poet *is* the nightingale. Inspiration à la John Keats is felt intuitively, sympathetically and at the very core of the human condition. No wonder that neither his Bodhisattva heart nor his weak lungs could immunise against the intensity of the world seen through his twenty-something eyes. In the end, Keats' star shone too bright.

Married Muses: Ted Hughes and Sylvia Plath; John Lennon and Yoko Ono

Ted Hughes and Sylvia Plath: Dark Star

'...the White Goddess is anti-domestic; she is the perpetual "other woman," and her part is difficult indeed for a woman of sensibility to play for more than a few years, because the temptation to commit suicide in simple domesticity lurks in every maenad's and muse's heart,' Robert Graves, *The White Goddess*.[25] According to Lucas Myers, fellow poet to Ted Hughes and Sylvia Plath and the 'go between' for their first orchestrated meeting, Ted Hughes was reading Graves' masterpiece on muses at the time that he met Plath, having received it as a matriculation gift from his mentor and teacher while at grammar school. According to Graves, any poetry inspired by the White Goddess is an expression of both exaltation and horror. And so, from the very beginning of the brief courtship between Hughes and Plath – which lasted just 112 days before they married – Plath was destined to play agent to the bewitching White Goddess.

Plath's first poem was in print at the age of eight in the

Boston Sunday Herald in the same year that her father Otto abandoned the family, racked with illness: terminal diabetes coupled with a gangrenous leg. This event haunted Plath for many years, and some literary biographers believe that Sylvia never truly got over his leaving but her absent father provided ample subject matter for much of her poetic output, which was mostly published and admired after her early death. Hughes was also a tremendously important agent for Plath's inspiration and her progression as a poet.

Despite each other's obvious reciprocal influence and inspiration during their seven-year marriage, Ted did not call Sylvia his muse – this was reserved for one of his later lovers, Jill Barber. But the creative couple worked in very close quarters, latterly sharing a cottage with two young children, often writing and typing on the reverse of each others' drafts. One of Sylvia Plath's biographers, Diane Middlebrook, describes their union as 'one of the most mutually productive literary marriages of the twentieth century'.[26]

Their first meeting could not have been dreamt up by a Hollywood screenwriter, although it has now been immortalised on film by Daniel Craig as Ted and Gwyneth Paltrow as Sylvia in the movie *Sylvia* (2003). Plath was on a two-year Fulbright fellowship at Newnham College, Cambridge, reading English, and Ted was a recent graduate in Social Anthropology from Pembroke College when they met at a party in Falcon Yard, Cambridge, in 1956. Plath already knew Hughes by reputation; she had read some of his work in the university literary magazines – and liked it. She had thrown herself into the Cambridge way of life and made concessions to fit in to the academic atmosphere such as dyeing her platinum blonde hair a more sedate mousey colour. The night of the fated meeting between the two volatile poets, Sylvia was wearing her favourite scarlet head scarf in her muted hair to coordinate with a pair of bright red shoes. She was also wearing her most flirtatious and outspoken side, but this bravado was always slightly betrayed by a physical scar on her cheek from an attempted suicide three years before she arrived in Cambridge and by the psychological side effects it left behind. Plath had over-dosed on her mother's sleeping pills and hid in the base-ment of her family home, lying in a catatonic state for three days; the concrete on which her cheek lay left the mark which she would have no doubt powdered over a little the evening she met Ted in Falcon Yard.

Before going to the party, Sylvia downs several whiskeys for Dutch courage and arrives drunk. She asks other people in the party who the 'big, dark, hunky boy' is, the man who Sylvia writes in her journal the next day is 'the only one there huge enough for me'.[27] It is Hughes. He approaches Sylvia square on, and she shouts over the loud jazz music lines of his own poetry straight at him, lines which she has committed to memory. Ted yells back, in a voice that Sylvia writes 'should have come from a Pole "You like?"' and invites her to join him in a brandy. They back into the adjacent room, the door slamming behind them, and Sylvia downs a glass of brandy. In the privacy of the empty room, they continue to holler at each other about the university literary magazine – a review of Sylvia's own work had appeared in it – and about Ted's life in London, where he was earning ten pounds a week. Throughout they are stamping their feet on the floor, Sylvia screaming that yes, she is 'all there'. And then Ted kisses Sylvia roughly on the mouth, rips off her red hair band, her silver earrings and barks that he shall keep them. When he ventures to kiss her neck, Sylvia bites him on the cheek. Blood runs down his face. The next day she writes in her journal that she can now see how women 'lie down for artists' and that Ted is the one man big enough for her, big and strong like his poems. She is smitten.

At the time, Ted Hughes was with another girl and Sylvia was emotionally involved in a long-distance relationship with an American student from Yale called Richard Sassoon whom she had met during her undergraduate years at Smith College in Northampton, Massachusetts. In 1956, the year that Sylvia met Ted, Richard was studying at the Sorbonne in Paris. Related to the British poet Siegfried Sassoon, Richard was impish compared to Ted – just Sylvia's height and of slight build, nothing in comparison to the rugged, Yorkshire constitution of 'Ted Huge'. Over the Christmas holiday of the previous year, Sylvia had travelled to France to visit Richard and continue their fling; they sojourned in Paris and took a road trip along the Côte d'Azur on a scooter. All very romantic, but, where Richard excelled in academic dexterity, he fell short in matching up to Sylvia's erotic fantasy of the big, bulky man who would sweep her off her feet. In her journals, we learn that Sylvia had argued with Richard about something during the French vacation and that they had left each other on bad terms. She returned to Cambridge with the resolve not to contact him unless he showed signs of remorse: she feared being jilted. By the time that Sylvia met Ted in February, she was rueful for not having played the field during her first semester, and had made a resolution to say yes to any date that a Cambridge scholar might ask her out on.

Four months after their first meeting, Sylvia and Ted married on 16 June 1956 in Bloomsbury, London. It was a small ceremony and the only family member in attendance was Sylvia's mother, Aurelia. Soon after marrying, they went on a European honeymoon to France and Spain and then moved to America, where they found work teaching, juggling their writing careers between jobs and managing to escape to the odd writers' retreat in Yaddo. In 1959, they returned to England. By then, Ted's first collection, *The Hawk in the Rain*, had been in print for two years, thanks to Sylvia who had negotiated the contract with the publisher to get it in print. In England they eventually settled in Devon where Sylvia played mother to their two small children, Frieda and Nicholas.

Those years were intense, creative and tough. Two creative geniuses struggled to balance their new roles as husband, wife, father, mother, breadwinner, mythmaker and magicians both of the written word. There were times when Ted, who had an interest in the occult (he experimented with the ouija board, and the couple used to hypnotise each other) believed their union was telepathic to such an extent that he felt that, when writing, the two of them drew from 'a single shared mind'. In an interview with the BBC recorded in 1961, Hughes said that their imaginations led a thoroughly 'secret life'; Plath disagreed, 'I think I'm a little more practical'.[28]

The strain on their marriage was exacerbated when Sylvia discovered that Ted was engaged in an affair with Assia Wevill, who had been married three times, latterly to the Canadian poet David Wevill. In May 1962, the Wevills spent a weekend in the Devon countryside with Ted and Sylvia: the weekend that Ted fell for Assia. Like Sylvia, Assia was creative, but her ego was far less pronounced. Six weeks after that weekend, Ted went to London for a meeting with the BBC and met Assia, alone. By the end of 1962, Sylvia's fairytale marriage to Ted had ended but the tragedy catalysed a creative spurt which saw Sylvia eagerly writing *Ariel* with alacrity and self-confidence. On the publication of the collection, Hughes said of his union with Plath that 'we were like two feet, each one using everything the other did'.[29]

Ted found himself legally bound to see the literary career of his wife realised. For, when Sylvia committed suicide in the early morning of 11 February 1963, placing her head in the oven and dying of carbon monoxide poisoning, he became not only sole carer to their two small children, but also literary executor to his estranged wife. He decided to place this responsibility in the hands of his sister, Olwyn, who apparently detested Plath and, in her capacity as literary executor, went to great lengths to take the edge off those passages in Sylvia's writing which painted an unflattering portrait of her brother. Ted suffered further public scrutiny when Assia Wevill killed herself and their four-year-old daughter Alexandra Tatiana Elise (nick-named Shura) in March 1969.

Once Hughes's award-winning collection *Birthday Letters* was published in 1998, the reading public got their first true insight into Hughes's psychological battle with the loss of Sylvia. When *Birthday Letters* won the Whitbread Book of the Year award on 26 January 1999, Frieda Hughes collected the prize on her father's behalf and read a confessional letter by him in which he wrote about how strange it felt to have finally made public his secrets, and lamented the fact that he had not done so 30 years previously, an act which he thought might have freed up his psychological life. 'Even now,' Hughes wrote, 'the sensation of inner liberation – a huge, sudden possibility of new inner experience. Quite strange.'[30] Ted Hughes had died of cancer on 28 October 1998 in his Devonshire home, three months before receiving the literary award and one day after Sylvia Plath would have celebrated her sixty-sixth birthday.

Graves' comment about the muse's heart always harbouring the wish to take her life in simple domesticity could have been written just for Sylvia. The fragility of her ego, her manic search for a husband and the volatility of her relationship with her big, hunky boy created the perfect conditions for this sensitive poet to take her life by using the iconic kitchen stove, symbolic of the destiny of so many women of the post-war generation. Let her loose and she will run wild, but rein her in and the muse will surely suffer. At the height of their creativity, the relationship between these two iconic poets was symbiotic: they fed off each other. Separated from Hughes, Plath felt the void deeply and, where Ted could keep his chin above water and go on to survive the death of two lovers and his infant, Sylvia simply wasn't strong enough.

John Lennon and Yoko Ono: Dream We Dream Together is Reality

John Lennon's last major interview, before he was murdered outside his Manhattan apartment, was with David Sheff of *Playboy* magazine. It lasted several days and was often in the presence of his second wife, muse and descendant of a ninth-century Japanese emperor, Yoko Ono. Sheff asks Lennon whether it was Ono who inspired Lennon to write one of his political songs, *Revolution*. Lennon responds: 'She inspired *all* this creation in me. It wasn't that she inspired the songs; she inspired *me*,'[31] and Lennon compares living with his one and only Ono to living with a searchlight. Yoko Ono and John Lennon: the most celebrated yet criticised muse-artist couple to come together in the twentieth century.

Their meeting was not orchestrated; it happened by chance. One day John Lennon strolled into the hip Indica gallery, then at the heart of swinging sixties London and the epitome of cool, where the work of New York avant-garde artist Yoko Ono, member of the experimental Fluxus group, was having its British début. John Dunbar, co-founder of the Indica (and at the time partner to Marianne Faithfull, before she left him to be Mick Jagger's squeeze) had invited Yoko Ono to exhibit on the basis that her work intrigued him, the one thing he looked for when practising as curator.

Accounts from Ono and Lennon vary as to what their first encounter was – from Lennon we hear that he bit into one of Ono's installations, *Apple*, a Granny Smith on a plinth that was on sale for £200 and from Ono we hear that Lennon climbed a ladder to peer through a spyglass in black canvas which revealed the word 'yes' in tiny letters – but it is certain that Dunbar made sure to steer Yoko towards John, a potential patron. Lennon remembers that, at the time, Ono had only heard of Beatles band member Ringo, maybe because it was also Japanese for apple. Lennon got the humour of Ono's work straight away and, when they met again at the gallery opening of Claes Oldenburg, Lennon agreed to Ono's request that he would back the show she was putting on at the Lisson gallery, *Yoko Plus Me*.

At the time of their meeting, Lennon was married to Cynthia, and Ono had been involved in two major rela-tionships – with the Japanese musician Toshi Ichiyangi and with Anthony Cox, an American jazz musician and film producer, with whom she had had a daughter, Kyoko Chan Cox, in 1963 before separating a year later. While The Beatles were at the peak of their career and were in the studios writing and recording the bestselling *The White Album*, Ono was also on the ascendant as the one to watch in artistic circles. Lennon felt that their meeting was written in the stars but the Fab Four didn't receive Ono as warmly; in fact, according to Lennon they despised and insulted her. Neither did the media fall under her spell, and some still blame her for the split of the Greatest Group on Earth. When Lennon and Ono released their first joint album *Two Virgins* with a cover which showed nude photos of them, it was banned and the typical opinion of the tabloids was that Lennon had gone off his rocker.

Like many relationships between two creative people, the one between John and Yoko encountered problems along the way with John having an extra-marital affair with his assistant, May Pang. Lennon and Ono separated for 18 months in 1973 until Yoko thought that John was truly ready to return. The early seventies were a troublesome time for the two of them; The Beatles' split in 1970 was, fans thought, down to Yoko's possessiveness. When *Rolling Stone* magazine asked John Lennon if he would take being a Beatle back, John replied, 'If I could be a fuckin' *fisherman* I would!... It's no fun being an artist. You know what it's like writing, it isn't fun, it's *torture*.'[32] But Ono and Lennon did enjoy their own laughs as creative playmates and, through their art and music, they explored each others' personalities, eccentricities and political beliefs. From the famous honeymoon 'bed-in' of 1969 where the newlywed couple protested against the Vietnam war by staying in an Amsterdam hotel bedroom for a week talking to newspaper reporters, to the exhibition that Ono put on at the Everson Museum in Syracuse, New York, where she wrote invitations in disappearing ink, they made both art and the headlines. The film documentary *Gimme Some Truth: The Making of John Lennon's Imagine Album* (2000) goes some way to revealing Ono and Lennon's collaborative and competitive relationship, as well as Lennon's creative genius.

It was at an Elton John concert in Madison Square Gardens, New York in 1973 that John and Yoko were reunited after their separation. During their time apart, John had endured a period of heavy drinking, at sea without his soul mate, and Yoko realised that they really did belong together, but as equals. After experiencing several miscarriages and a course in Chinese acupuncture, Yoko gave birth to their only son, Sean Taro Ono Lennon, in 1975, and the roles were reversed: John became the househusband, Yoko the businesswoman – as Gala Dalí was to her Salvador. Perhaps this was Ono's way of making up for her own experience of an absentee father in early childhood in Japan; she did not meet her own father, Eisuke, a banker in San Francisco, until she was two.

In an interview with *Rolling Stone* magazine, Lennon says he saw Ono as his teacher, his 'Don Juan' and in response to the question if he had a picture of 'When I'm 64', Lennon replies: 'I hope we're a nice old couple off the coast of Ireland or something like that, looking at our scrapbook of madness.'[33] But this newfound familial bliss was short-lived, and John was never to see his sixty-fourth year. Leaving his Dakota apartment in the early evening of

8 December 1980 Lennon was shot dead, at close range and in sight of Ono, by Mark Chapman in an act which has since become a hub of interest to conspiracy theorists around the world. The lyrics written by the musical legend, who once said that inspiration is a game of letting go, have gone on to inspire generations of songwriters in his wake and, to this day, Yoko Ono continues fiercely to defend her influence on Lennon's musical career.

There was something intensely personal about Yoko and John: it was as if, even when they were apart, they lived with each other. The window into the intimacy of their union which they gave to the public was wide open; they seemed to welcome inspection, and to thrive on introspection. Ono's quote, 'Dream we dream together is reality,' sums up the effect of inspiration on this couple who did everything they could to manifest the landscape of their dream worlds through collaborating creatively. But, in a bold move, and in direct opposition to the familial model in which Sylvia Plath found herself, this maenad made it clear that the domestic was to have no influence in her domain. Ono was a muse who rallied against the maternal, just like Gala 'you can call me *merde* but don't call me *mère*' Dalí. The multidisciplinary make-up of the muse begins to fracture and, by shunning the role of mother, Ono assumed in its place the role of mentor and, latterly, manager of Lennon's memory.

Exotic Muses: Salvador and Gala Dalí; Henry Miller and Anaïs Nin

Gala Dalí: Gala *La Gale*

'For me,' Salvador Dalí is quoted as having said of his wife and muse, 'eating Gala would be the deepest expression of love.'[34] Born Helena Dimitrievna Diakonova in 1895, Gala would become the disloyal wife to the French poet Paul Éluard, the absent mother to their only child Cécile, and the source of many men's infatuations including the artist Max Ernst and the lead singer of rock band Black Sabbath, Jeff Fenholt. But the liaison for which she is best remembered is her 53-year relationship with the surrealist Catalan artist Salvador Dalí.

It was on holiday in Cadaqués in Spain that Gala Éluard met Dalí, and in true surrealist style, the 25-year-old artist went to great lengths to make an impression. He took a knife to his finest silk shirt and shaved off the bottom, wore his swimming trunks inside out to expose the stains on the lining, dyed his armpit with a mixture of fresh blood and blue laundry powder, and dabbed at his neck with a concoction of fish glue and goat manure. The final flourish was a red geranium which he placed ceremoniously behind his ear.

Gala was 35, promiscuous, impressionable, an *agent provocateur,* known for her short temper and her eyes, which Éluard said could pierce walls. If someone annoyed her, she would think nothing of burning their flesh with a lit cigarette. Dalí, then in the early days of his surrealist career, made the impression he had hoped for – although he did tone down his outfit before introducing himself. Gala and Dalí became inseparable during the Spanish holiday and, when Éluard left, she stayed behind to be with her 'little boy', but not before Dalí had painted Paul Éluard's portrait. Dalí wrote in his memoirs, 'I felt it incumbent on me to fix forever the face of the poet from whose Olympus I had stolen one of the muses.'[35]

Dalí had a lot to prove. He had been named after his brother whom his mother had deified and who had died just a couple of weeks before Salvador was conceived. Gala would become his manager in order to realise the success which he felt had thus been bestowed upon him. The relationship between the two exhibitionists was rocky: Dalí had an absurd fear of female genitalia and Gala had a high libido to satisfy so pursued numerous flings. The two volatile characters lived in extreme conditions, sometimes in dire poverty and sometimes in exhibitionist luxury, and desperate events became the source of Dalí's inspiration. In his memoirs, Dalí describes how, in 1931 when Gala was having a fibrous tumour removed from her uterus (which was to leave her infertile), he returned alone to their apartment in Paris 'inspired like a musician: new ideas sparked in the depth of my imagination'.[36] At this stage of their relationship, they had only been together for a short while but Dalí had already become dependent on her presence and prescience. He was at risk without her; during one famous lecture in London, he almost suffocated in a heavy copper diving suit. Dalí and Gala would remain together for over five decades, although Gala was far from faithful during their partnership; despite her matrimonial duties, she had many affairs.

Gala passed away on 10 June 1982 in Port Lligat, in the house which Dalí had designed and built as their retreat, not far from Cadaqués where the couple had first met. Even Gala's death betrayed the eccentricities which became the hallmark of the surrealist movement: she had written in her will that she wished to spend her final days down the road in their castle in Pubol and be buried there in her favourite red Dior dress, but it was against Spanish law to move a corpse until a judge had examined it. On finding Gala's dead body, her chauffeur, Arturo located Dalí to tell him the sad news, but Dalí, convinced that she would never die, didn't believe she was truly dead. Once he realised that his muse had indeed passed away, he and Arturo stripped Gala, wrapped her in a blanket and put her in the back of their Cadillac. This was then to be driven to Pubol, together with a nurse, in case the car was stopped by police and they could then claim that Gala had died on the way to the hospital.

Dalí outlived Gala by seven years and eventually died on

23 January 1989. His wife's body, and especially her back, has become synonymous with surrealist art. In one *trompe l'oeil* exercise by Dalí, the hourglass figure of Gala's nude body, turned towards the Mediterranean becomes, at a distance, a portrait of the American president Abraham Lincoln. Although she was never to bear Salvador any children, Gala becomes the Madonna of Port Lligat, complete with infant, in a well-known portrait from 1949. The fragmentation of objects on the canvas in this oil painting represents the nuclear mysticism which prevailed in many of Dalí's canvases, and speaks more to the atomic experiments at Hiroshima in the mid-twentieth century than to motherhood. Perhaps this is appropriate for a woman whom Parisian art dealers referred to as *la Gale* – in colloquial terms, a nasty piece of work or, in medical speak, an irritating itch. After all, this was a woman for whom the maternal instinct was redundant; Gala refused all contact with her own daughter, Cécile.

There were likely to be few compatible life companions for an artist like Dalí, possessed of such extremes of temperament, such insecurities to heal and such a larger than life ego in need of indulging. No wallflower or retiring violet could have made such an impression on one so vulnerable and yet bloody-minded. This coupling was like-for-like; Gala gave as good as she got and ultimately the pair became defined through their relationship with each other. To be without the semi-divine Gala was like being without oxygen for Salvador, and yet she did a pretty good job in restricting his supply at times – Gala's extramarital wanderings may have been to the detriment of their marriage, but the inspiration and provocation that she provided was instrumental in catalysing some of the most daring artistic works of Dalí's time.

Anaïs Nin: All for the Sake of the Dream

'I write these words: "On *being* the womb." And it unleashes a tremendous feminine universe. I am completely divorced from man's world of ideas. I swim in nature. On *being* the womb... englobing,'[37] Anaïs Nin wrote in March 1937. Nin wrote her voluminous journal from the age of eleven, when she was on a ship sailing from her native France to America with her mother. She filled a volume a year, and stowed the books safely in a bank vault in Brooklyn at a cost of $53 a month: she knew they would eventually earn back the cost when they were published.

Like Gala Dalí, Anaïs Nin was larger than life: extravagant, erotic and iconic in the landscape of twentieth-century feminism. Her striking appearance – due to her mixed ancestry which included forebears from Cuba, France and Denmark – was characterised by black hair, even and slim eyebrows and a European sense of style. Nin became muse to the American writer Henry Miller, whose best known works include *Tropic of Cancer* and *Tropic of Capricorn*. Again, like Gala, Nin intoxicated many men with her sensuality; her lovers included the twice-married Henry Miller, the writers Edmund Wilson and Gore Vidal, the Austrian psychoanalyst Otto Rank, pupil and then close colleague of Sigmund Freud – even her own father. Nin had a complicated relationship with her father who had walked out of the family when Anaïs was in early adolescence and her relationship with him would be closely examined by psychoanalytic circles, not least because one of Anaïs's books was called *The House of Incest*.

Nin married Hugh Guiler (known to Anaïs as Hugo), then a New York banker and latterly a lithographer and filmmaker, when she was in her late teens. After marrying, Nin returned to France to finish the manuscript of her first book, *DH Lawrence: An Unprofessional Study*, a mature study of the English author which was published in 1932. It was during this writing retreat that she met Henry Miller, in the autumn of 1931. Miller was also mid-manuscript – while Anaïs was writing from the luxurious surroundings of a house in Louceviennes, he was working on the first draft of *Tropic of Cancer* in dire financial straits. On the face of it, Miller and Nin had little in common other than their shared love of literature. They were very different 'breeds' of writers: Miller was concerned with the outer world, the empirical; Nin was obsessed with the inner, with Freud's burgeoning unconscious and with expressing the inexpressible and the transcendent. But a strong bond was formed on both the physical and the intellectual plane and it was a bond which would last for over three decades and see Nin sacrifice clothes, shoes, curtains, books, writing paper and even her own typewriter for Miller's literary accomplishment. The first publication of *Tropic of Cancer* was backed by Nin as the publisher, Jack Kahane of Obelisk Press, concerned about its controversial nature, vacillated for over two years.

France became 'mother, mistress, home and muse'[38] to Henry Miller and Anaïs was also a critical means of support over the years. Although the factual accuracy of Nin's journals is debated by critics, they remain an insightful source into the intricacies of this artist-muse relationship. So too do Henry Miller's letters which have a similar status as a literary accomplishment. In them, Miller and Nin correspond about writers they admire and include carbon copies of writing experiments, criticisms of each other's work, embryonic manuscripts, corn plasters, menus, glass bottles and publishing contracts. Miller even includes details of his diet and urinary habits. Hurried letters and telegrams sent from France, Switzerland, Corfu and America convey intimate thoughts about the human condition, reading recommendations and offers of help and money from Nin when Miller's bank balance reaches a low ebb.

Within the first year of meeting each other, Miller writes to his confidante from Lycée Carnot in Dijon: 'Cultivate the madness. Do not run from it. In madness there is wisdom for the artist. Let everything go to the head and let it boil there.'[39] Throughout the letters, there is a sense of the urgent pressure to write; Miller writes that the gas cocks are open and that he is writing like a steam engine under the influence of inspiration. He thanks his muse for exciting him, for being his critical pair of eyes. On her part, Nin had a razor-like ability to drill down into the core of personalities. She writes of Miller in her journal that, 'He denies the life of feeling which he corrodes by angers, contrariness, denials and role-playing, by fragmentation, dispersion. Henry's definition of human is the one who drinks, forgets, is irresponsible, unfaithful, fallible. Mine is the one who is aware of the feelings of other human beings.'[40] And Lawrence Durrell, a friend of both Miller and Nin, writes of Anaïs's fecund nature and sensuality, 'We are all writing about the Womb, but you are the Womb.'[41]

This idea of being attracted to the source of life within people is central to Nin's character and arguably what attracted so many creators to this 'englobing' and deeply intuitive muse. One of Nin's other more enduring relationships was with the camera-shy actor Rupert Pole, to whom she was married bigamously for 11 years towards the end of her life. She kept this marriage secret from her husband Hugo, ingeniously creating a complex 'lie box system' in her handbag which included different compartments for her cheque books under the names of Anaïs Pole and Anaïs Guiler. Rupert and Anaïs first met in an elevator en route to a party in New York, and weeks later she accompanied him across the continent from the Big Apple to the City of Angels where she set up an entirely separate and concurrent life to the extent that, when she died of cancer in January 1977, the *LA Times* and the *New York Times* ran different obituaries.

'"She loved too much." This could be on my tombstone,' Anaïs wrote in her journal.[42] In death, Anaïs wished to be remembered as one who had sacrificed all for the dream. For Miller, the writer should remain humble in the realisation that his life and his particular faculty for using his 'antennae' to pick up the words dictated to him is in service to others. 'He has nothing to be proud of, his name means nothing, his ego is nil, he's only an instrument in a long procession.' This muse-artist couple seemingly had vastly different approaches to the creative process and yet the attraction between the yin and the yang fostered a long-standing and sustainable friendship and was a critical means of support for Miller.

It is hard to imagine what artists' lives would have been without their muses: would Miller have ever attained the literary success he did without Nin? What would Dalí have painted in place of Gala's back? Often disarming, always essential, muses suggest just enough encouragement and provocation to tease the work out of the artists: something as simple as a woman's silhouette can inform a lifetime's artistic output.

Mutual Muses: Vincent Van Gogh and Paul Gauguin; Wordsworth and Coleridge

Vincent Van Gogh and Paul Gauguin: No Blue Without Yellow

In the spring of 2006, *L'Arlésienne,* a painting by Vincent Van Gogh, sold at auction for over £22 million – the fourth highest price for any of Van Gogh's works. The masterpiece, which took Van Gogh just 45 minutes to execute, was created in homage to Paul Gauguin. The French painter was not only sharing a house with Van Gogh at the time of its composition, but was also sharing the same sitter, Madame Ginoux of the Café de la Gare, during a nine-week retreat with Vincent in his Yellow House.

Van Gogh remained obscure during his short life, selling only one painting – *Red Vineyard at Arles* – via Theo, the younger brother who was at once his art dealer and most ardent supporter, with whom Vincent corresponded frequently. 'So Gauguin is going to join you, it will mean a great change in your life,' Theo wrote to Vincent on 19 October 1888[43] and, four days later, at sunrise, the French artist Paul Gauguin arrived in Arles. The idea of Gauguin joining Van Gogh for an extended artists' retreat had taken eight months to realise since Gauguin first asked Vincent if he would put in a good word to Theo on his behalf in February. The plan took shape: Gauguin was to move into the Yellow House, sending a painting a month to Theo as payment in kind for accommodation, sustenance and painting materials.

Gauguin vacillated before agreeing and the prolonged wait for Gauguin's arrival both frustrated and inspired Van Gogh. In anticipation of Gauguin joining him, he entered a white heat of creativity, churning out paintings at an astonishing rate and, when his mouth wasn't occupied by his pipe, downing endless cups of coffee and hunks of bread. He paid little attention to his bodily needs, apart from the odd visit to the water closet, the brothel or the Café de la Gare for an absinthe to take the edge off the caffeine. But the love-in with Gauguin would be short-lived. Gauguin left for Paris on Boxing Day only nine weeks after arriving, on learning that Van Gogh, in what he defended as simply an artist's fit, had sliced off his left ear. They would never see each other again.

For most of their claustrophobic residency, the two neurotic artists spent the best part of 24 hours in each other's company, drawing and painting the same rustic, contemporary subject matter, sharing artistic advice, visiting brothels together, and drinking absinthe before eating at home once they had decided to save money by no longer taking their meals at the nearby Restaurant Venissat. Gauguin cooked except for one meal, a soup, which

Gauguin found intolerable; he guessed that Van Gogh had not followed any recipe but thrown the vegetables together for their aesthetics rather than for their complementary flavours.

This was a frenzied period for Van Gogh; he wrote that pictures came to him 'with a terrible lucidity at moments... I am hardly conscious of myself and the picture comes to me like in a dream.'[44] In the studio, which they shared, two artists with very different styles of working struggled to accommodate each other's eccentricities. Whereas Gauguin was precise and took time over his quiet composition, Van Gogh would paint with passion, slapping blocks of colour onto the canvas with bravura, spending over 14 hours a day in front of his easel. 'We painters,' he wrote to fellow artist Émile Bernard, 'must get our orgasms from the eye.'[45] It was in Van Gogh's nature to experiment; painting a new portrait was a process of discovering new ways to communicate through colour. One of the last paintings he executed before Paul Gauguin's long-awaited arrival had been a self portrait: his red hair is razor-short, his gaze disturbingly penetrative and the background a vivid green, swirling around Van Gogh's head in his distinctive style, avant-garde for the period. It is dedicated to his fellow painter with these words 'à mon ami Gauguin'.

In his letters, which are adapted by the writer Irving Stone for his book *Dear Theo*, Van Gogh writes to his brother, 'I am ashamed of it, but I am vain enough to want to make a certain impression on Gauguin by my work, so I

cannot help wanting to do as much work as possible before
he comes. His coming will alter my way of painting and I
shall gain by it.'[46] In many ways the residency was doomed
to failure from the beginning, despite all of Vincent's best
intentions. Gauguin's biographer, Charles Estienne, points
out that the works of the artists are poles apart and that
these were the very magnetic poles that initially attracted
Van Gogh and Gauguin to each other, and then violently
repelled them. We can see this destructive magnetism
work in other 'mutual musing' instances: take Sylvia Plath
and Ted Hughes or, on the flipside, take John Lennon and
Yoko Ono's love-in as an example of a creative partnership
which, despite its ups and downs, essentially produced an
impressive output of artistic work, albeit of mixed merit.

The decline of Vincent's mental state, culminating in his
slicing off his left ear, is well-known but the circumstances
leading up to this event – and Gauguin's role in them – are
perhaps less familiar. Vincent was in a self-proclaimed state
of painting like a steam engine, and his relationship and
reliance on his new-found friend was intensifying. In the
days leading up to the self-mutilation, Vincent was seen
throwing a glass of absinthe at Gauguin in the café during a
particularly heated argument. In order to patch up their
quarrel the pair decided to take a break from the studio
and visit the Bruyas Collection in the art gallery in
Montpelier. There, they discussed their respective opinions
and the yawning gap between their professional tastes
served to only rupture the relationship further. It was
around this period in December that Vincent wrote to

Theo that 'Gauguin and I discuss Delacroix, Rembrandt, etc., a great deal. The debate is exceedingly electric, and sometimes when we finish our minds are as drained as an electric battery after discharge.'[47]

The fuse blew on 23 December 1888. According to Paul Gauguin's and Johanna Van Gogh's accounts, the sequence of events went something like this: Gauguin goes for a walk through the gardens in La Place Lamartine to escape, no doubt, the atmosphere of the Yellow House only for Van Gogh to sneak up on him, threatening him with a razor – maybe the same which would later serve to sever Vincent's ear. Gauguin calms his colleague by talking rationally to him and then decides that the sensible option may be to take leave of Van Gogh and the Yellow House for the night and to find shelter at a local hotel. The next report of Vincent's late-night activity comes from the brothel. Vincent arrives, asking after his favoured prostitute, Rachel, as he has a gift for her safe-keeping: a slice of his own ear complete with strict instructions that Rachel should look after it carefully. Roulin, the postman (and subject of one of Van Gogh's studies) accompanies Vincent back to the Yellow House and the police later discover Vincent unconscious in bed, lying on blood-soaked sheets, and he is hospitalised.

Loyal Theo came to the rescue on receiving a telegram in Paris and stayed with Vincent over the Christmas holiday. Vincent's mental state only declined over the months that followed before his death by suicide on 29 July 1890. Gauguin's reaction to hearing of Van Gogh's suicide was distant: 'Sad though this death may be, I am not very grieved, for I knew it was coming and I knew how this poor fellow suffered in his struggles with madness.'[48] Gauguin didn't write about Vincent's self-mutilation until fifteen years had passed and yet his nine weeks with Van Gogh are known to have produced one of the most experimental periods in his oeuvre.

This creative coupling exemplifies the alluring and magnetic power of muses at their most potent – and harmful. Although the pairing inspired Van Gogh greatly, it was the beginning of a sentence in his life which ended in the ultimate full stop. The enthusiastic friendship which the retreat promised to foster soon faltered, along with Van Gogh's grip on reality. The veil between genius and insanity is very thin, and those artists who manage to lift it for long enough to be inspired by the madness but short enough not to be consumed by it, are among those who produce the most exciting works. A nobody in his own lifetime, Van Gogh is the epitome of inspired madness: the seam he drew his inspiration from was rich, but crazed, and Gauguin gave him the licence to dig a little too deep.

Wordsworth and Coleridge: A Lyrical Collaboration

The natural world has been a source of inspiration for many centuries, but appreciation of nature enjoyed a particularly widespread renaissance in the era of the Romantic poets in the late eighteenth and early nineteenth centuries. This period bred many outstanding writers who earned their place in the literary canon – Southey, Lamb, Hazlitt, Byron, Keats – but there are two poets and one collection in particular which stands both as a testimony to the power of nature to inspire and to the magic of mutual musedom: William Wordsworth and Samuel Taylor Coleridge's collection from 1798, the *Lyrical Ballads*.

This unique 'joint experiment', as the two poets liked to refer to it, was the result of a decision that the two took when out walking in Alfoxden, in the Quantock Hills in Somerset, during March 1798, three years after they had first met each other in Bristol. Just three months later, in June, the pair would have the manuscript complete, bar two poems. One of Coleridge's most celebrated biographers, Richard Holmes, makes the point that this collection was dreamt up in a climate of sensibility in which a 'New Man of Feeling' openly expressed his emotions, opinions and feelings towards his fellow male friends.[49] He would weep, laugh, debate, drink and dine in his friends' company – perhaps the New Age man of 200 years later is not such a revolution.

True to form there was also a woman whose role it was to open further the eyes of the pair: Dorothy Wordsworth, William's somewhat overbearingly loyal sister and the object of Coleridge's admiration. Coleridge described the platonic love that existed between him, Wordsworth and Dorothy in terms of sharing the same soul and his wife, Sarah Coleridge, didn't really get a look-in. Dorothy has been credited with teaching both her brother and Coleridge the critical faculty of *seeing* in its fullest sense:

seeing nature deeply and closely and coupling that with the poetic and sensitive imagination – what Wordsworth and Coleridge were best at. For Wordsworth, the imagination is 'that intellectual lens through the medium of which the poetical observer *sees* the objects of this observation, modified both in form and colour',[50] and the poet should trust his sensations to guide him to the place in which he will find true inspiration. For Coleridge, who subsequently composed a whole treatise on fancy and the poetic imagination in his quixotic *Biographia Literaria,* the 'esemplastic imagination' is an assimilating energy, a synthesiser of experience and sensation and the ideal poet 'diffuses a tone, and spirit of unity, that blends (as it were) *fuses*, each into each, by that sympathetic and magical power, to which we have exclusively appropriated the name of imagination.'[51] (Readers can be forgiven for not knowing what Coleridge meant by 'esemplastic', for it was a word that he invented in order to best convey that sense of 'shaping into oneness'.)

For the collaborators of the *Lyrical Ballads*, common man and his language would be their muse – or, in Wordsworth and Coleridge's own words from the 1800 *Preface*, they chose to portray low and rustic life. (Political correctness wasn't, of course, *de rigueur* in those days.) The poets chose to look at the lives of the lower classes because they had not been sidelined by the stresses of urban living, had a more immediate and passionate connection with their earthy environment and possessed a simpler, more straightforward vocabulary. It should not be forgotten that to use common man as muse was rather radical in the 1790s; no Western European poet had ever really waded this far into the lives of rustic folk, their concerns and habitats.

When they began their collaborative project, Coleridge already had a collection of poems to his name, published in 1796, and Wordsworth had likewise established himself as a man of letters. What made them stand out in their contemporary literary circles was their approach to writing the *Lyrical Ballads* – the innovative qualities of composition which they brought to bear on the *process* of writing it. They stressed that true poetry was the 'spontaneous overflow of powerful feelings' which took its origin in emotions recollected in tranquillity.[52] And the 'tranquillity' is the important part: good poetry is not just about a knee-jerk outpouring of emotions or observations all at once but rather it is meditative, the poetry being filtered quietly onto the page. In his poetical 'system', Coleridge made a distinction between imagination and fancy whereby imagination's role is to respond to inspiration mechanically, and with an element of measured choice. As Coleridge would later write in *Biographia Literaria*, portraying rustic life and language was an attempt to tap into the '*lingua communis*' – what a Jungian would most likely refer to as the collective unconscious.

The supernatural, faith, repentance, solitude, reincarnation, exile: in the *Lyrical Ballads* these themes crop up repeatedly but each has its ultimate source in nature. Of his four contributed poems, only one of Coleridge's was technically a ballad and it is also among the most critically acclaimed ballads of the collection – the *Rime of the Ancient Mariner*.[53] The poem began to emerge in earnest when Coleridge and Wordsworth went on a long wintry walk in Somerset which took several days and started at dusk on 13 November 1797. Originally begun as a collaborative poem, it soon became obvious that the literary possessor of the gothic *Ancient Mariner* was Coleridge, although Wordsworth did contribute some structural ideas for dramatic interventions during their hike. Coleridge had been turning over images of the supernatural and a spectre ship in his imagination for years, with influences dating back as far as the ballads he heard in infancy. The poem took him about five months of intense and increasingly inspired writing to complete and stands as a testament to the power of nature over mankind, the mariner's fatal shooting of an albatross setting off a chain of events which causes the ship's crew to thirst, wither and crumble under the intense heat of the sun. Coleridge not only earned his poetic sea-legs with this ballad, he also pulled off a magnificent feat of inspired storytelling.

William Wordsworth's contribution to the *Ballads* was more meaty for a simple reason: his poetic output was speedier and, as a collaborator, he was more inclined to put his views forward strongly and to take more of a leading role in steering the project. Wordsworth wrote most of his poems in the spring of 1798, his poems erring less into the territory of the supernatural than Coleridge's. In the final edition of the *Lyrical Ballads,* Wordsworth contributed the majority of poems: nineteen compared to Coleridge's four.

Creative collaborations between artists can be prone to combustible conflicts of interest, but mutual musing, in the right conditions, can have a powerful catalysing effect. Where Van Gogh and Gauguin favoured absinthe and brothels, Wordsworth and Coleridge got their kicks from long hikes through rural Somerset. What is fundamentally similar, however, in these instances of mutual musedom, is the meaningful meeting of minds. For those with a predisposition to manic tendencies, this intellectual marriage can become too much – an obsession – yet the intoxicating alchemy can still serve to inspire masterpieces. Although Coleridge and Wordsworth's relationship also suffered its ups and downs – often due to Coleridge's opium addiction – the partnership sustained itself well beyond Van Gogh's and Gauguin's mere nine weeks.

In the ultimate manoeuvre of honouring the inspirational friendship which Wordsworth shared in their poetical double act, he dedicated to Coleridge what would become his most famous poem, posthumously published, *The Prelude*. And in the *Biographia Literaria,* Coleridge would reflect on literary friendships in general that, 'the writings of a contemporary, perhaps not many years older than himself, surrounded by the same circumstances, and disciplined by the same manners, possess a *reality* for [a young man], and inspire an actual friendship as of a man for a man.'[54] The understanding which the aspiring writer finds in the work of his or her contemporaries offers a safe haven where he can connect with his inner world. The co-inspirational relationships between the two romantic poets and the Dutch and French painters were, in their own unique ways, co-creations of new cultural realities expressed through the medium of the written word and the loaded paint brush.

Fated Muses: Dante Gabriel Rossetti and Lizzie Siddal; William S. and Joan Burroughs

Dante Gabriel Rossetti and Lizzie Siddal: How They Met Themselves

In German folklore, to meet one's doppelgänger is a sign that one's death is imminent. Dante Gabriel Rossetti's painting *How They Met Themselves*, which represents two lovers in medieval attire in a dark forest meeting their doppelgängers, foretells the tragic events which would unfold in real life two years after it was completed, for the two couples are modelled on the artist and muse: Rossetti himself and Lizzie Siddal.

One of the women seems weak-kneed, faltering in the clutch of the man by her side, her hands out in front of her, zombie-like. Her pale complexion, drooping eyelids and half-open mouth betray signs of illness or imminent fainting. This is the canvas which Rossetti began in 1851 but did not finish until his honeymoon with his muse, Lizzie Siddal, in 1860. Lizzie had been waiting years for Rossetti to ask her to marry him and his proposal was finally guilt-induced for, by the late 1850s, Lizzie's health, which had never been good, was failing badly. The couple conceived a child in the year of their marriage but, tragically, it was stillborn. Lizzie's addiction to the tincture of opium known more commonly as laudanum, widely prescribed in the Victorian era to combat many ills, including depression, was probably the cause of her child's death and certainly the cause of her own self-induced death in 1862, two years after their honeymoon.

The drawing is symptomatic of the relationship between Lizzie and Rossetti. In Lizzie, Rossetti felt he had met his destiny and it's easy to understand why he became so intoxicated by her presence, for Lizzie was simply stunning. Tall, with beautifully structured cheekbones, a radiant mane of copper hair, porcelain complexion with a tint of rose, and wide-set, luminous eyes – Lizzie was the Pre-Raphaelite equivalent of the modern supermodel, the epitome of everything for which painters from the Pre-Raphaelite Brotherhood were searching. Lizzie was immortalised in dozens of Pre-Raphaelite drawings and paintings, most notably in John Everett Millais' *Ophelia* (1852) which depicts a drowned Ophelia lying face up in the river, with meadow flowers floating about her open palms. In ominous anticipation of her own death, Lizzie almost contracted pneumonia when posing for this portrait; the candles which were keeping the water warm in the tin bath in which she was lying had gone out, but Millais was so absorbed in the composition that he failed to notice. Lizzie was numb with cold when she finally made it out of the bath but, as her role as model dictated, had quietly and professionally persisted in lying deathly still despite the freezing cold water.

Many painters from the Pre-Raphaelite Brotherhood relied on patrons to support their work and Dante Gabriel Rossetti was no exception. The writer and artist John Ruskin patronised Rossetti, which won him support through much of the 1850s until Rossetti tired of the restrictions which this financial and advisory support brought to bear upon his own artistic interests. Ruskin was acutely aware of how important a model Lizzie was to the artist, and at one time wrote that she cured Rossetti of all his worst faults when the artist looked upon her. Later, Ruskin would worry that Lizzie's ill health was negatively affecting Rossetti's artistic output and so he made arrangements for Lizzie to recuperate in the south of France. He then offered to provide the money to fund her marriage to Rossetti in order to solidify their union, which had been on shaky ground. Rossetti's sister, the poet Christina Rossetti, never approved of her brother's relationship or marriage to Lizzie. Rossetti would be so distracted by his muse that at times, despite having commissions of other subject matters to work on, he would instead relentlessly draw Lizzie. His contemporaries noted that Lizzie was a distraction, but one that he could not bear to be without. Rossetti was obsessed.

Just as Lou Andreas-Salomé would suggest to Rilke that he change his name from René to Rainer because Lou thought René sounded too precious, Rossetti urged Lizzie to drop the second 'l' in her surname (she was christened

Elizabeth Eleanor Siddall) in order to shroud Lizzie's working class background; she was working as a milliner's assistant when she was first 'spotted'. However, the psychological baggage which Lizzie bore from early childhood would not be as easy to dismiss. Her physical ill health was undoubtedly brought on by her mental instability, as well as her tendency to wallow in morbid thoughts and revel in her melancholic disposition. Mrs Kincaid, who accompanied Lizzie on recuperating trips to Europe, is said to have remarked that Lizzie's illness was a product of her own imagination and her doctor, Dr Acland, concurred. However, Lizzie's presence and aura should not be underplayed: those who met her were sure to be struck by not only her beauty but also her gracious nature. Unfortunately her overall loveliness was not enough to keep Rossetti's eyes from wandering, and he had dalliances with other women and with other Pre-Raphaelite models including the blonde-haired and beautiful Miss Annie Miller. We see this infidelity replicated in other muse-artist relationships – take Ted Hughes and Sylvia Plath, for example, or look at Gala's promiscuous affairs. Living with the knowledge of Rossetti's infidelities provoked such immense jealousy in Lizzie that it only worsened her nihilistic tendencies. Eventually, Lizzie, like Sylvia, committed the irreversible act of self-destruction: suicide.

At her burial in Highgate cemetery in 1862, Dante Gabriel Rossetti stood by her plot and pleaded with Lizzie to return to him. In a macabre way, she did. Seven years after the burial, Lizzie's plot was dug up at night under

Rossetti's orders and her coffin exhumed, in order to recover a volume of his unpublished poems he had placed inside it among other keepsakes. Rossetti's agent Charles Augustus Howell attended the exhumation and reassured the distraught Rossetti that Lizzie remained as perfectly luminous in death as she had been in life. Her copper hair, Howell said, had continued to grow in her grave and filled the coffin, glowing by the flaming torches which were illuminating the ghostly proceedings. The exhumation was worth it; Rossetti earned £800 in the first year after publishing the volume, *Poems*, which included those from the coffin. But the act of re-opening Lizzie's grave came at a larger psychological cost and it haunted Rossetti for many years afterwards. Howell's account of her pristine corpse, albeit make-believe, would turn Lizzie Siddal into an iconic, ghostly and mythical figure in the history of the Pre-Raphaelite movement.

Beyond death, Lizzie was still muse to Rossetti. His painting *Beata Beatrix* (1864–70) was not completed until well after her burial. In this painting, Lizzie's pose is struck on the cusp of death; she sits with her hands open on her lap and a little bird is dropping a poppy into her palm. The beloved's hooded eyes are closed and her chin is cupped upwards in expectation of transition to heaven. The masterpiece was inspired by Dante's *La Vita Nuova* and it almost never made its way onto the canvas, as Rossetti's assistant Henry Treffry Dunn explains in a charming little book, *Recollections of Dante Gabriel Rossetti and his Circle*.[55]

Rossetti's agent Howell intervened when he saw that

the canvas for *Beata Beatrix*, on which the painter had already marked out and completed the head and the hands, was in danger of being damaged and forgotten at the back of his studio. One day, when Howell found himself in the studio without the artist, unbeknownst to Rossetti, he retrieved the canvas to have it relined and repaired. The artist was so traumatised by Lizzie's death that previously he could not bear to contemplate returning to the painting, but Howell slowly convinced Rossetti that it was worth trying to finish, which he did. However, by the time *Poems* was published and *Beata Beatrix* was complete, Rossetti had reached a period of great mental instability. In 1872, ten years after Lizzie's death, Rossetti suffered a nervous breakdown from which he would never fully recover. The breakdown was partly precipitated by the adverse reaction he received from the publication of the disinterred *Poems*, and his last decade, until his death in 1882, Dante Gabriel Rossetti spent in seclusion.

There is something compulsive and vaguely vulgar about Rossetti's dependency on his muse: he magnetised Lizzie toward him, fed hungrily from the inspiration with which she provided him and then rebuffed her when she got too close. Rossetti's concern for Lizzie vacillated and it seems it was easier and more productive for him to remain just out of her reach. The twist which Rossetti maybe did not expect was that, in the end, Lizzie's tacit power over him in death was more potent than his control over her in life. Perhaps Rossetti believed it might have been easier for him to cherish the memory of his raven-haired beauty than to live with her fading glory, greying locks and decrepitude. But Rossetti found out a little too late that he actually needed Lizzie alive as much as he needed daylight to paint by.

William S. and Joan Vollmer Adams Burroughs: The Dead Star

6 September 1951. Joan Vollmer Adams Burroughs and her common-law husband William S(eward) Burroughs are at a party in a friend's apartment above his bar called the Bounty in Mexico City. Gin has been drunk as if it is water and it's getting late when William suggests to his wife that it is time for their 'William Tell act'. Obligingly, Joan balances a highball glass atop her head and turns her face away from her husband – she doesn't like the sight of blood, she says. Burroughs takes aim with his Star .380 automatic from six feet away, misses the glass and kills his 27-year-old wife outright.

Joan Burroughs was central to the Beat revolution which swept America in the mid-twentieth century. Her friends and fellow Beat writers included Jack and Edie Kerouac, Herbert Huncke, and her husband and accidental murderer, William S. Burroughs. Joan Burroughs was like a candle – she drew people in with her magnetic intelligence, natural inquisitiveness and, especially, her bohemian attitudes and lifestyle in a highly conservative post-war society. She found her way to New York City to study at Barnard College as soon as she could leave the claustrophobic surroundings of suburban Loudonville, in the upper reaches of New York State. In the Big Apple she met and married a law student, but soon flew that matrimonial nest for the comfort of strangers and moved into an apartment with Edie Parker, the then girlfriend and future wife of Jack Kerouac.

Joan met William S. Burroughs, known as Bill, through mutual friends in her shared apartment. The place she lived in with Edie Parker quickly became a melting pot of radical writers and those who railed against the status quo. Joan fell for Bill, despite the fact that he preferred men and was a self-confessed misogynist who thought that women may well have been a biological mistake. From early 1946 they began living together, sharing their psychic connection, deepest thoughts and, soon, addiction to drugs: Bill became hooked on heroin, Joan on the drug Benzedrine. This didn't stop them starting a family and buying farmland in Texas from which they vowed to start a new life but on which they would grow marijuana. Even a move out west would not put an end to their narcotic-fuelled life and, on being caught making out in public by a sheriff, they fled to New Orleans rather than face the penalty Bill received for drink driving and public indecency. The law kept up with them, however, and, after being charged in the next state for possession of drugs, the couple moved again, this time across the border to the relatively lawless Mexico City.

After the fatal William Tell act of September 1951, Burroughs spent just 13 days in jail. He met his legal fines of $2,000 and bail of $2,313 and walked free. But the guilt associated with shooting his common-law wife never left him, and in fact it fuelled his inspiration after her death. *Naked Lunch*, Burroughs' first novel and one which was sexually explicit, came out eight years later. Its publication caused a stir, the stream of consciousness book was temporarily banned and Burroughs stood trial for its obscenity (he didn't mention, of course, that he had written most of it under the influence of marijuana). Burroughs openly confessed that, if it were not for killing Joan, then he may never have penned the book, or even become a real writer. The reality of what he had done never left him: '...the death of Joan brought me in contact with the invader, the ugly spirit, and manoeuvred me into a life long struggle in which I have had no choice except to write my way out.'[56]

Burroughs' work enjoyed an underground following, but opinions of the celebrity author varied: in the eyes of Norman Mailer, Burroughs was a genius but many journalists branded him a pornographer, a sensationalist, a junky. After Joan's death, Burroughs wrote with the intention to alter and expand states of consciousness within himself; he believed that a writer was essentially 'a mapmaker of psychic areas',[57] and Burroughs lived for almost half a century in the shadow of Joan's death under which he became a cartographer of the inner life. Burroughs 'wrote his way out' of Joan's death well into the mid 1990s, and just three years after his own passing in 1997 the biopic *Beat* was released with Kiefer Sutherland playing Burroughs and Courtney Love as Joan.

The dance between destruction and creation is a delicate one. Where Dante Gabriel Rossetti could hardly bear to return to his easel after Lizzie's suicide, Burroughs sought solace in his typewriter after Joan's burial. The kind of boozy, intoxicated lifestyle that Joan and Bill enjoyed in the forties would have been seen in ancient Greece as Dionysian, playful but potentially destructive. Burroughs' ability to steer his troubled soul through the years immediately after shooting Joan catalysed an unparalleled and unorthodox creativity. The life and times of inspirers like Lizzie and Joan may not be a bed of roses but, if the artists can handle the energy which their muses' being and passing engenders, then their works may flourish against all odds.

Iconic Muse

Rainer Maria Rilke and Lou Andreas-Salomé: You Alone are Real to Me

Known to Freud as 'the great understander', Lou Andreas-Salomé was a writer, the ultimate independent woman, a thinker who exuded a kind of sexy intellectualism. In 1887, Lou married Friedrich Carl Andreas, a professor of Persian, but their marriage remained unconsummated and, once her sexuality fully blossomed in her thirties, Lou took on a string of lovers. Lou was muse to many – Friedrich Nietzsche, whose proposal of marriage Lou refused, the philosopher and writer Paul Ree, the psychoanalyst Sigmund Freud – but she was especially indispensable in the life and work of the poet Rainer Maria Rilke.

Rilke and Lou's bond was beyond lust – even love – a link on the level of the subliminal. Salomé writes in her account of Rilke, *You Alone Are Real to Me:* 'Two halves did not seek completion in each other. But a surprised whole recognised itself in an unfathomable totality. So then we were rather like primal siblings, before incest had become sacrilege.'[58] The poetry of Rainer Maria Rilke slices through the superfluous and incidental details of life to the core of our very being. His was an unparalleled courage to see into the heart of things which took him to the very edge of human nature where the veil between this life and the transcendent is paper-thin. And it is Rilke's prowess in communicating this through his poetry that has made his work timelessly popular. His motivations to write were not dissimilar to the muse Anaïs Nin who wished to travel to the centre of people and 'is-ness', although Rilke, arguably, pulled this off with more sincerity, less ego and, in turn, more suffering.

Lou, who was born and bred in St Petersburg, met Rilke on 12 May 1897 in Munich, when they were introduced by the writer Jakob Wasserman. Lou's work was already known to Rilke, who had read and admired her essay *Jesus the Jew*, one essay out of a considerable literary output which also included two novels, *Ruth* and *Searching for God*. Their friendship would span three decades, include a four-year love affair, and influence Rilke to change in subtle and not so subtle ways. It was Lou's idea that he change his first name from René to Rainer and Lou's biographer Heinz Frederick Peters[59] remarks that, once the two had met, Rainer's handwriting changed noticeably from an illegible, sloppy hand to one which was precise and presentable, just like Lou's. In one of the surviving letters from Rilke to Lou during the halcyon days of their early affair, Rilke writes: 'I want to be you... I do not want to do anything that does not praise you... I want to be you.'[60] Theirs was an unmistakably energetic connection: the meeting of two bright sparks.

From Munich the couple travelled to a small rented house in the mountain village of Wolfratshausen accompanied by Frieda von Bülow and August Endell. In the early summer sun, Lou and Rilke would walk alone through the garden barefoot, Lou teaching him names of the flowers, berries, insects and birdsong, Rilke listening attentively and learning, through her eyes, to really see. It was during this time that Rilke's poetic voice matured to a point where he began to express his feelings with beautiful simplicity. For Rilke, Lou was the older, wiser woman (the age gap between them was 14 years, and he was only 22 years old when they met) and she became the centre of his world, the rock he relied upon when the pressures of carving out a career as a poet became too intense. Lou was the perfect candidate for the role of muse for Rilke: she had the mindfulness and sensitivity to reach out to him at a level beyond words. As the Swedish psychiatrist Poul Bjerre wrote of Lou: 'She had the gift of entering completely into the mind of the man she loved... Like a catalyst she activated my thought processes.'[61]

Lou travelled with Rilke to her native Russia twice during their affair and, on one occasion, Lou's husband even accompanied the pair. On the second trip, relations between Lou and Rilke faltered and Lou suggested a separation in which she went to Schmargendorf and Rilke went to write in an artists' colony in Worpswede. The letter Rilke wrote after their affair came to an end commemorates their period of togetherness as one of rich productivity, due to Lou, 'The transforming experience which then seized me at a hundred places at once emanated from the great reality of your being. I had never before in my groping hesitancy felt life so much, believed in the present and recognized the future so much.'[62] Lou and Rilke later took the decision to destroy the love letters between them from that era, but Lou's inspirational effect on Rilke can still be sensed through his poetic progression.

It was the turn of the century and the promise of a new age inspired Rilke to start a new life. And so, in April 1901, he married Clara Westhoff, a sculptor whom he had met on his writing retreat. The marriage, however, did not flourish and, when Rilke went to Paris to write a monograph about the sculptor Auguste Rodin, he refused to return to his wife and newborn daughter, Ruth. It was the years *after* his separation from Lou which saw Rilke's poetry spawn and blossom to its fullest potential which it reached in the 1910s and 1920s with sequences such as the *Duino Elegies*, the *Sonnets to Orpheus*, and the so-called 'thing' poems which were, in part, influenced by the poet's time in the Parisian *Jardin des Plantes* while he was working for Rodin. Once Rilke saw Rodin at work on his sculptures, he felt moved to work for him, and Rodin, whose motto was *'il faut toujours travailler'* ('one must always work'), took him on as secretary.

Rilke and Lou's epistolary relationship after their physical one had come to an end offers a unique insight into the growth of the poet and his concerns. Rilke's letters were penned all over Europe: from the Spanish town of Ronda to Paris, from the Italian capital to Duino Castle (Rilke had a liking for living in castles and fortresses). Writing eloquently and with complete honesty about his work, Rilke confides in Lou about his creative process, his philosophy on life and the struggles he encountered with his health (Rilke was never of a strong constitution and was fairly miserable during his compulsory military service). He outlines his next writing projects, asking her for her feedback, and includes poems for her and drafts of prose to be read and critiqued. In response to one letter to Lou,[63] Rilke clutches her missive to his breast, and writes that he is like a headless ant and that Lou can see the anthill on the horizon, and thus comfort Rilke that the journey is not in vain. Lou is Rilke's homecoming. She is his vision.

In this sense, Henry Miller's relationship with Anaïs Nin echoes that of Lou and Rilke's: the roles that Rilke asked Lou to take on through writing to him – as mother-figure and confidante – are not dissimilar to the expectations Miller had of Nin. Rilke clearly needs reassurance and looks to Lou to qualify his career, as if she is the possessor of his poetic licence: 'Somehow I must get down to the making of things,' Rilke writes. 'Somehow I too must discover the smallest element, the core of my art, the tangible yet insubstantial technique for expressing all things...'[64] In his letters to his muse, readers sense the exhausting, arduous life of the artist, living outside the system and inside the mind where Rilke questioned life in the plainest terms of what it means to be, in Nietzsche's words, human, all too human.

Rilke's self-realisation reached its apex during a retreat

in Duino Castle on the Adriatic coast in early 1912, during which time he 'delivered into existence' – a phrase Rilke used for composing – one of the greatest cycle of poetic elegies of the twentieth century, the *Duino Elegies*. From October 1911 until May 1912, Rilke stayed in a quiet room in the corner of one of the castle's wings which over-looked the crashing winter seas, and wrote. There he was hosted by Maria von Thurn und Taxis-Hohenlohe with whom he would execute translations of Dante's *La Vita Nuova* at night. Her account of Rilke's outstanding poetic genesis is that it started on 21 January 1912 but the ten elegies, which took him just a few days to draft, would not be completed until after the First World War.

This watershed marked a new chapter in Rilke's devel-opment as a poet. Inspirational energy took possession of him: 'It was a hurricane, Everything in me that was fibre, texture and framework has cracked and bent,'[65] Rilke wrote to Lou in February 1912. On the day of the elegies' inception, Rilke had gone for a walk in the high winds along the battlements when he seemed to hear, in the strong Bora wind which gusted above his head, the line of verse, 'Who, if I screamed would hear me then, out of the ranks of the angels?' Rilke realised that such a great influx of inspiration could provoke a similarly grand reaction somewhere deep in his psyche, but he was determined to reach his potential as a poet, and not get 'in the way' of the art. Rilke returned to his room and let the words flow from the gifted first line which became the opening to the first *Duino* elegy. Of all the great poets, Rilke is among those who understood at the deepest level what it meant to be a conduit to the work itself; as such he could decline nothing, he was 'incurably exposed'[66] and it was Lou's role in their friendship to protect him as best she could from the elements, and from himself.

For Lou, Rilke was 'the first real truth',[67] the man in whose presence she felt secure enough to express herself with sexual and intellectual ardour. Although the older of the two, Lou outlived Rilke, passing away at the age of 75 and leaving an impressive literary and intellectual legacy in her wake. If Lou was Rilke's sight-giving eyes, periscoped above the anthill precipice, Rilke was her heart. One gets the sense from reading Lou's memoirs of Rilke's life *You Alone Are Real to Me*, that Rilke was, at times, as much muse to Lou as she was to him. It is clear that Rilke's ability to sustain himself as a poet during his life was largely indebted to Lou's capacity to be his great understander and to be, if not always the origin of his inspiration, at least the ears and the eyes for which he wrote until he died of leukaemia at the end of 1926, aged 51.

It was in the year after his death that Lou wrote the memoirs of her Rilke which reveal only fragmented insights into their subliminal union. Lou writes of the poet's inspiration and such a lifelong need to exist that he felt compelled to prove himself daily through his toilsome writing, through trusting everything, through paying respect to all experience, be it good or bad. Ultimately, Rilke felt compelled to prove himself through acknowledging the differences that 'so urgently and seductively tear us apart in highs and lows, triumphs and failures, heaven and hell, life and death'.[68] Lou's muse relationships with other contemporary luminaries like Friedrich Nietzsche and Sigmund Freud are similarly fascinating to read about; she is possibly one of the most widely acclaimed of all the muses covered in this book. In fact, an entire volume could be written just about Lou in her role as multi-faceted muse, but a whole chapter on her in this short guide will have to suffice.

Infant Muses

Ian and Caspar Fleming; James and Lucia Joyce; Charles Lutwidge Dodgson and Alice Liddell: Pure, Unclouded Brow and Dreaming Eyes of Wonder

It has been the destiny of many children to inspire their parent or playmate to create a work of artistic genius. Ian Fleming is renowned for the James Bond stories which have now all reached the silver screen, yet one of his most popular stories has nothing to do with Her Majesty's Secret Service, Aston Martins or Martinis. During a recuperative spell in 1961 at the Dudley Hotel in Hove, in the south of England, Fleming was inspired to write a story suitable for his son Caspar to read.[69] The result was *Chitty Chitty Bang Bang: The Magical Car,* the popular children's story, first published in 1964 and later transformed into a successful film with Dick Van Dyke playing the lead Caractacus Potts in 1968, and then into a West End and Broadway musical in the early 2000s.

A more destructive muse-artist relationship between adult artist and child muse is that of Irish writer James Joyce with his daughter, Lucia, who was born while Joyce

was writing *Portrait of the Artist as a Young Man*. Joyce
thought his daughter was extra-special, a fantastic being
who relished living in the imaginative and creative realms
with which he was so preoccupied. In *Lucia Joyce: To Dance
the Wake*, Lucia Joyce's biographer, Carol Loeb Shloss[70]
explains how Lucia was instrumental in inspiring Joyce
while he composed *Finnegans Wake*, a book which would
come to define the era of modernist literature. The
primary resources about this child muse are scant but some
facts are known: that she suffered from strabismus (crossed
eyes); that her early childhood was particularly itinerant
but that she finally settled into the Parisian way of life and
joined an avant-garde dance troupe there, thus finding a
mode of expressing her troubled self through movement.
It is known that Lucia ended up in hospital after her
brother checked her in for chucking a chair at their mother
on James Joyce's fiftieth birthday. Lucia was then trans-
ferred to an asylum in Ivry, outside Paris, at the age of 28.
She never left the confines of a mental institution again
before her death in 1982 aged 72.

But arguably the most famous infant muse is Alice
Pleasance Liddell who inspired the eccentric Charles
Lutwidge Dodgson, better known as Lewis Carroll, to
write *Alice in Wonderland,* a fairytale he started telling one
perfect summer's day in Oxford. Common to all infant
muses – and, arguably, to all muses in general – is what
Dodgson described as a readiness to accept the 'wildest
impossibilities with all that utter trust that only dreamers
know'.[71] Born in May 1852 to the Dean of Christ Church

in Oxford, Alice had ten siblings, including two younger brothers called Arthur and Albert who died in their infancy. Alice is perhaps most associated with her two elder sisters, Lorina and Edith, since Dodgson often photographed her with them. (Charles Dodgson was also an avid photographer; in fact he was one of the most celebrated portrait photographers of the era.) A son of a clergyman, Dodgson was most comfortable in the presence of little girls and it was only then that his stammer would disappear. Nowadays, Dodgson would probably be classified as suffering from, at best obsessive-compulsive disorder, at worst paedophilia. He had strange ways about him including the tendency to write in purple ink, to walk bolt upright and to be so punctilious about knots that he wrote his publishers, enclosing diagrams of how string securing any parcels containing manuscripts sent to him should be tied. Controversy still surrounds the question of whether or not Dodgson was a paedophile, although there is no clear-cut evidence to support claims that he was. Whatever the truth about this, his penchant for photographing little girls was certainly class-sensitive and it is said that he didn't ask children from the working classes to pose for him, for fear of photographing their unattractive thick ankles.

Dodgson may have been a pedant but he always possessed the ability to capture the imagination of children, mainly because of the entertainment tasks bestowed upon him as the youngest boy in a family of ten children. And the Liddell girls provided Dodgson as an adult with exquisite models for his portraits, and willing little ears for his make-believe stories. The 'golden afternoon' of 4 July 1862, the afternoon that *Alice's Adventures in Wonderland* was conceived, has since been immortalised in the annals of children's literature.

Alice, along with her sisters Lorina and Edith, Dodgson and the Reverend Robinson Duckworth, were enjoying a boating trip along the River Isis and the prospect of a picnic at Godstow Lock in Oxford. The three little girls begged Dodgson to tell them one of his fairytales. He acquiesced but played with them throughout the telling, pretending to fall asleep mid-sentence and saying it was time for bed. It was Alice's role to plead with Dodgson to write down the fairytale so that she and her sisters would be able to enjoy it again. In this way, Alice became the creative catalyst for the psychedelic story set in topsy-turvy wonderland. From the iconic illustrations which have accompanied the story for so long, we are led to believe that Alice had long blonde locks and blue eyes but, in reality, Alice Liddell had fine brown hair, cut to a conservative shoulder length. The inspiration for Alice in the illustrations had come from Sir John Tenniel, the *Punch* cartoonist who provided drawings for the original manuscript. Dodgson had given Tenniel a photo of another little girl, the doll-like Mary Hilton Badcock, with instructions not to replicate the *bona fide* Alice in his interpretation of the wonder-child.

Writing to the dramatist Tom Taylor, Charles Dodgson ran through the options for the book title:[72]

Alice among the	{elves Alice's {goblins	{hour {doings {adventures	{elf-land in {wonderland

and the final version of the manuscript is much embellished in comparison to the simple fairytale with which Dodgson regaled the Liddell children that famous July afternoon. In his essay *Alice on the Stage*, Dodgson reveals the creative process through which he conjured up his kaleidoscopic world. Alice's request for the story to be written down was the catalyst but the story itself proceeded to take on a life of its own, Dodgson adding 'many fresh ideas which seemed to grow of themselves', ideas which sometimes came to him involuntarily at the dead of night or when he was out on a walk in a winter landscape. Dodgson remembers that he had no notion of what to do with his inquisitive heroine at the outset of the story so he decided, with little sense of what would happen next, to send her straight down a rabbit hole. One thing about Dodgson's inspiration was predictable, however: 'whenever or however it comes, it comes of itself. I cannot set invention going like a clock.'[73] This was not inspiration on demand, but one which had its home in a wide-eyed child with enough curiosity to kill the cat.

Dodgson's relationship with his maiden muse came to a surprising end in 1863 and mystery still surrounds the missing pages from Dodgson's diary in which entries about the enchanting Liddell sisters come to an abrupt end. Many people have speculated about the reasons for the severing of the relationship and theories proposed have included that Dodgson was involved with the family's governess, that there was a falling out between Alice's father and Dodgson, and that Alice's mother disapproved of Dodgson taking such a devoted interest in her daughters. In any case Dodgson continued with the manuscript of *Alice*. He completed it in February 1863 and watched as it went on to be a fairy tale which intrigued children and adults alike around the globe. The real life Alice Pleasance Liddell, later Liddell Hargreaves, went on to become the recipient of an honorary doctorate from Columbia University but, some time before receiving this accolade, she had auctioned off her original copy of the hand-illustrated manuscript in order to get her errant son out of financial troubles.

Little wonder that little children can hold the key to the brainwaves of many a writer. Seeing things not as they are, but as they could be, children have an imagination elastic enough to make believe that the plastic bottle they hurl across the room is a space rocket or the ointment in the little bottle is actually a marvellous medicine that will make them shrink to the size of a pea. That utter trust which, Dodgson wrote, is inherent in a child's conception of reality is just the kind of trust which severely degenerates as the child turns into an adult; the cubist artist Picasso once said that every child is an artist and that the problem is how to remain an artist once the child grows up.

Lewis Carroll sat very comfortably in the company of children: like many children's authors, he had a Peter Pan-like imagination which never wanted to grow up. One hundred and one years after Lewis Carroll's death, his namesake, an American author Lee Carroll and co-author Jan Tober published a book called *The Indigo Children: The New Kids Have Arrived*. It has gone on to sell over a quarter of a million copies and explains a phenomenon that mothers and fathers around the world today are starting to notice with more frequency: that their children seem to have new and undocumented ways of behaving, belief systems and ways of being in the world. Indigo children, Carroll and Tober explain, arrive in the world with a feeling of royalty, and of deserving to be alive. Easily frustrated with systems that don't require creative thought, they are quick to see alternative and better ways of doing things. It is believed that indigo children are here to show adults how to heal the world and enter a new paradigm of reality. One can only wonder if the children's author who wrote in indigo ink and sent his young protagonist down a rabbit hole to take tea with a Mad Hatter and receive advice from a caterpillar smoking a hookah atop a mushroom, was an indigo adult, a century before his time.

Twenty-first
Century Inspiration

Lindsay Clarke, Theodore Zeldin and Sara Allan:
A Contemporary Novelist, Thinker and Artist on
Today's Inspiration

Society has moved on apace since the days of the Ancient Greeks and, although our appreciation of inspiration may have changed, our understanding of it has not been particularly well finessed. In the modern technobabble culture of constant change, the quality of patience demanded by divine inspiration is becoming rare. 'A good poet is someone who manages, in a lifetime of standing out in thunderstorms, to be struck by lightning five or six times; a dozen times and he is great,'[74] the poet Randall Jarrell once said and yet we live in an age which views the unfamiliar with suspicion and which honours immediate gratification above all else.

Some of those contemporary artists patient enough to hang around for those bolts from the blue to strike were interviewed in March 2006 by the psychoanalyst Adam Phillips in a cover feature for the *Observer* 'Review' section called *My Inspiration: What Inspires Us?*[75] In Phillips's mind, inspiration is 'a kind of God-term; it refers to something we think of as essential but that we can't, or may not want to, understand,' and yet despite not being able to conceptualise inspiration better Phillips says we now 'glamorise' inspiration and 'idealise' those artists possessed by it.

For the musician Beth Orton, her magical muse is inanimate; it's her second-hand Levin acoustic guitar. Orton sometimes thinks the Levin has locked inside it all the songs she's ever written since she got it. The contemporary artist Cornelia Parker compares inspiration to a microscopic jigsaw puzzle with 'tiny points of stimulus accumulated over time [that] come together in an instant, making you think you have had an idea that came from nowhere'. And for both the dancer Akram Khan and the film director Pawel Pawlikowski resonance is key: they know that they're onto a good thing when something inside themselves chimes with the outside world and in that moment, 'my ancestors,' Khan believes, 'start to whisper to me.' Spooky stuff and yet this concept of the inner harmonising with the outer is seen by many as central to the nature of inspiration.

In an interview, the novelist Lindsay Clarke, author of *The Chymical Wedding,* said that this magical marriage between the inner and outer can culminate in an experience where 'one is admitted, however briefly, into the privileged realm of *soul* where there is no evident division between oneself and everything else – hence the feeling of possession, of being possessed'.[76] Over the years of being a writer, Clarke has become more aware of the role that the living earth has to play in inspiration, and that the intelligence of the planet may be the principal source of inspiration. Given that the origin of the archetypal Greek muses was the marriage of Gaia (the earth) and Ouranos (the heavens), this is perhaps unsurprising. Ken Wilber's nobly-titled book *The Theory of Everything* agrees with Clarke's concept and explains that this journey to the heart of the matter happens when one manages to lose the ego: '... when, in nature, you can relax your egoic grasping and stand as an opening or clearing in awareness... then through that clearing might come pouring the power and the glory of the World Soul, and you are temporarily struck perfectly dead by the wonder and the beauty of it all...'[77]

Musedom in the twenty-first century is being used for different ends. The Oxford professor, philosopher, historian and writer Theodore Zeldin set up the Oxford Muse Foundation in 2001 in order to bring together people who want inspiration to think more imaginatively, to cultivate their emotions through practice of the arts and to understand the past better and to have a clearer vision of the future. In essence, Zeldin's is a bid to democratise the muse and make her accessible to everyone. Based on a belief that people have a basic need to be inspired and encouraged, the Muse project runs conversations over dinner around the world to bring together everyone from civil servants to school teachers, business leaders and the underprivileged to share their views of the world and learn from each other in an atmosphere free from hierarchy. On the menu is a framework of conversations which creates

the conditions for people to focus on what is most important in their lives. To trigger this conversation and process
of self-realisation, people around the dinner table are asked
to draw their own self-portraits and include in the picture
whatever they want the world to know about them.

In Zeldin's eyes musedom has many practical benefits
which are ripe for the picking in the twenty-first century:
he believes that, by harnessing the potential to catalyse
inspiration in others, it is possible for people to be freed
from any enslaving conditions which minimise their
personal potential. It is important to widen the horizon,
through inspiration, of those who have received a narrow-
minded education. To this end Zeldin set up an MCA, a
course which reaches beyond the MA to enable students to
learn about radical differences in thinking across a large
cross-section of cultures and disciplines.

In the book for which he is perhaps best known, *An
Intimate History of Humanity,* Zeldin writes about the
provenance of the chemical catalyst in 1835 when Baron
Berzelius of Stockholm introduced the term into the
chemist's vocabulary. Berzelius realised that combinations
of two separate substances often vitally depended upon a
third party. This discovery raised the status of catalysts to
a much higher level, giving them an existence and a *raison
d'être* independent of those substances which they fused
together. Almost 200 years since they were discovered,
still nobody quite understands how chemical catalysts
work. Zeldin explains that 'It used to be thought that they
remained unchanged during reactions, but it is now

believed they absorb a small portion of the substances they transform', and that now scientists have come to realise that intermediaries may need other intermediaries present in order to kick off the reaction process. In other words, the world is based upon a whole series of interactions.[78]

Not only do we privilege immediate gratification in the new millennium, this is an era which is increasingly solipsistic, or individualised. The reminder that third parties, catalysts and intermediaries are just as valid and essential is a timely one. Zeldin describes intermediaries as heroes who open up the world and who are able to keep in their sights all the many dimensions of reality. Intermediaries are able to focus all at once on the personal, the local and the universal. The comparison between muses and intermediaries is a close one: in many ways, muses are the unsung heroes and heroines of the artistic world, the invisible and unquantifiable energy which often isn't name-checked in artists' acknowledgements, or roll-called in their award acceptance speeches. Perhaps fittingly, inspiration seems not to want to be recognised: remember fey George Yeats's preference to hide in the shadow of the limelight surrounding *A Vision*, Lizzie Siddal's quiet slip into catatonia, or Joan Burroughs' turn of her queasy head as her husband took aim. One contemporary artist who has begun to understand inspirational energy and musedom at the expense of her ego is Sara Allan.

Allan works as a 'channelling artist' and believes that the unconscious can dictate a work of art without the intervention of a preconceived aesthetic doctrine. Her guide Emmanuel, whom she refers to as her muse, inspiration and energy, directs Allan's hands across the canvas so that she draws a series of lines both curved and straight. Her hand then wavers across a palette of over 50 pure colours which is chosen from by the same energetic intervention. Allan's artistic style has been described by the British jazz musician and art critic George Melly as 'automated surrealism' and isn't a world away from the automatic writing process experienced by George Yeats. In fact, at the end of the process of painting the canvases, which can often be as wide as seven feet, Allan signs her initials, SEA, and then writes the painting's title automatically. The finished works, which are abstract and made up predominantly of geometric shapes and bent lines in bold colours, are not dissimilar to the works of Miró or Picasso.

Emmanuel, who Allan has gleaned through writing with him is from the twelfth century, is also known to be the source of inspiration for an American author and a musician. Emmanuel's work, through Allan, is to produce what he calls a magnificent series of 12 paintings, denoted by the zodiacal signs, which are for the youth of tomorrow and may not necessarily be understood by the painter's contemporaries. What is particularly striking in talking to Sara Allan about the painter's role in the guided creative process is the extent to which she lets her ego be sublimated. She recognises that she may not appreciate immediately the beauty of what Emmanuel (a name which traditionally means 'God with us') is creating and that, as

Emmanuel says, today we have a man-made conception of beauty.

Not a small amount of preparation, courage and patience was necessary to get Allan's craft and spirit to the point where she could let go masterfully enough to commence this catalytic project. In fact, it was during a particularly sorrowful stage of her life that the self-effacing Sara Allan found solace and a new direction in this auto-mated work. Love energises the mysterious process, she explains, and Allan has no intention of demystifying it: Emmanuel instructs her to love the mystery.

This mystery began to deepen one exhibition not long after the year 2000 when a physicist in the gallery approached Allan, pointing to her painting *Being An Artist in the Studio*. This piece, painted predominantly in cobalt blue and mauve tones, depicts a female artist at her easel. The physicist was brandishing a picture of high-energy particles colliding taken in 'bubble chambers' by the CERN labora-tory. It bore an uncanny resemblance to the canvas. *Being An Artist in the Studio* was painted by Allan in complete ignorance of the experiments in particle physics during the latter half of the twentieth century. But what this synchronicity begins to hint at is that the world of physics, art and inspiration may be far more related than we have ever believed.

The Future of Inspiration

May the Muse Be with You

The archetypal muse has adapted over millennia from her origins as a mountain goddess and yet she remains just as multi-faceted, endlessly mysterious and infinitely nebulous. Inspiration remains elusive, but might our restricted understanding of the muse-world and our inability to pin down the nature of inspiration have something to do with the paradigm of reality through which we explore and explain these amazing bolts from the blue? Our philosophical and scientific heritage in the West favours dualism and reductionism, and our reality predominantly remains one in which effect will always follow cause and two plus two will always make four. Yet our lived experience of the world doesn't always match up to the logical code of conduct which Newtonian science or Cartesian philosophy dictates, particularly in the realm of inspiration and creativity. There is something inherently magical about muses and intriguing about inspiration: coupled with the right artist, muses can midwife a work of art that seems to come straight from a divine spirit, and inspiration can invoke a poem which will stir the hearts and imaginations of readers the world over.

This final chapter explores what happens when we examine musedom through the lens of the emergent quantum world, a world defined by our participation in relationships, which favours an interdisciplinary, holistic outlook and which provides an extraordinary synthesis between the cutting edge of Western scientific thinking and the ancient wisdom and teachings of the East. Quantum physics presents us with a smörgåsbord of such possibilities as being able to be in two places at the same time and the interconnectedness of everything in the universe. By contextualising muses and inspiration within just a few aspects of this science, the nature of inspiration may begin to reveal itself in a new light. Those readers less acquainted with the vocabulary and technical understanding of quantum physics need not fear for this is aimed not at an academic audience, but at the curious and open of mind.

Before examining muses within the realm of the quantum world it is worth putting the chapter in the context of the work of the writer and scientist Leonard Shlain whose in-depth study *Art and Physics* tracks, side by side, the ascendance of new artistic expressions and the trajectory of discoveries in modern physics in order to bring to the surface the relationship between the break-throughs in each of the two fields. Shlain discovered some-thing very interesting: revolutionary art precognitively anticipates visionary physics. First comes the avant-garde artist and his new way of understanding reality on his canvas which foreshadows the work of the physicists who make unprecedented leaps in the understanding of the physical world, using new scientific theories which echo what artists had already predicted and pioneered years before.

Shlain's study reveals that there is a zeitgeist in each age that the artists and the physicists are both tapping in to and that, despite working contemporaneously in this spirit, the two professions have very little appreciation or understanding of each other's practice. Shlain takes cubism as an example: the work of Pablo Picasso from 1907 to 1910 radicalised the way in which space and mass were realised on canvas by breaking up images into pieces and then rearranging them so they no longer followed a linear time sequence and then arranging these bits on a backdrop of broken Euclidean space. Picasso saw himself as an artist as 'a receptacle of emotions come from no matter where: from the sky, the earth, a piece of paper, a passing figure, a cobweb. This is why one must not discriminate between things.'[79] This groundbreaking work was created before Einstein had published any of his articles on relativity theory which also shattered the four tenets of Newtonian physical reality: space, time, mass and energy. These four discrete entities became two, namely the space-time continuum and the energy-mass equivalence. Time and space are no longer absolute in either Einstein's or Picasso's interpretation of the world. In Einstein's new world view space *is* time and matter *is* energy and, by the time Einstein formulated it, Picasso's work was already calling into question all those pre-conceived ideas of reality to which man had become so accustomed. Sara Allan's *Being an Artist in the Studio,* created in isolation of any knowledge about CERN laboratory work of colliding atoms in a bubble chamber, is a modern example of an artist tapping into this pervasive zeitgeist.

Quantum physics similarly demands that we re-perceive the fundamental way in which we engage with the world. In the quantum paradigm, solid matter is no longer the static stuff we believed it to be – it is moving, unpredictable, and here by virtue of being observed. Space is not empty but full of invisible energy bizarrely buzzing about us. Everything is entangled and exists because consciousness has intended it to be. In the quantum climate of intention, the integral qualities of a muse to excite and inspire the energy for a work of genius to be produced may well be performing much more of an important task than is usually assumed.

Inspiration and Energy Fields

The nineteenth-century writer and critic Matthew Arnold wrote that, 'Genius is mainly an affair of energy, and poetry is mainly an affair of genius; therefore, a nation whose spirit is characterised by energy may well be eminent in poetry.'[80] Energy is something which, in the Newtonian paradigm, was customarily associated with kinetics, thermal energy and electromagnetic radiation. In the twentieth century however, psychologists started to take human energy into account when creating their theories and practice. CG Jung, for example, recognised that a person's energy was central to psychology, and it had an intensity that could be measured to a greater or lesser degree.[81] Until the concept of a field was struck upon, scientists of the time struggled to explain the effects of gravitational and electromagnetic forces.

In its various incarnations, Field Theory is now proving invaluable as we probe the micro and macro mysteries of the universe. Recently, scientists have furthered our knowledge of something called the Zero Point Field which they describe as an ocean of energy, subatomic vibrations in the space between things which connects everything in the universe.[82] This field can be quantitatively measured, and causes what is known as the Casimir effect. According to the Field principle, the universe is dynamic and constantly in energetic exchange between the cobweb of energy which envelops it. Theodore Zeldin has a complementary idea of an encompassing cobweb which he sees as connecting individual human beings like a combination of filaments which stretch across the frontiers of space and time:

> Every individual assembles past loyalties, present needs and visions of the future in a web of different contours, with the help of heterogeneous elements borrowed from other individuals; and this constant give-and-take has been the main stimulus of humanity's energy.[83]

Frontier science, transpersonal psychology (which was born out of Jungian theory) and leading philosophers of the day seem to be portraying a world in which an invisible 'sea' of energy is out there and in here, dynamic, filled with potential and creativity. It wouldn't take a massive leap of the imagination to extend this visualisation to encompass an energetic source of inspiration which muses and artists are plugged into, and some frontier scientists have even suggested as much.

Zero Point Energy is a manifestation of sub-atomic 'fuzziness' caused by the constant creation of fundamental particles that are briefly flitting into and out of existence. The theory holds that for any vibration there remains a small residual energy which is rooted in the quantum uncertainty principle, even at a temperature of absolute zero. Communication, if measured by vibrations, is therefore taking place even at the level of the subatomic world. Field scientists have discovered that communication between cells and DNA, for example, occurs through frequencies and that human brains also contribute to, and are influenced by, this world of waves. This idea is often linked to telepathic experiences and phenomena such as the collective conscious: simply put, when two or more people are on the same wavelength. Some scientists have even suggested that our more sophisticated cognitive processes result from interacting with the Zero Point Field and that this might go some way to account for our intuitive and creative capacities 'and how ideas come to us in bursts of insight, sometimes in fragments but often as a miraculous whole'.[84]

Uncertainty is a big feature of quantum physics and it

was most famously explored by the prodigal son of quantum science, Werner Heisenberg, whose earliest published theory of quantum mechanics came out when he was just 23. Heisenberg was concerned with that which can be observed: the energy emitted by an electron changing state, for example. His controversial and seminal paper describing his Theory of Uncertainty sent shock-waves through the scientific community when it was published in 1927. Broadly speaking Heisenberg's theory states that, for a moving particle such as an electron, the more precisely one measures the position, the less exact the measurement of its momentum (mass times velocity), and vice versa. It is impossible to know both accurately at the same time – an uncertainty that Gnostics would have perhaps found much more bearable. The acceptance of this theory was another nail in the coffin of the traditional Newtonian view of the universe which had long held that physics described a world that was absolute, endlessly measurable and predictable. The state of the universe, according to quantum mechanics, is not embedded in the present, rather it is taking part in a great game of chance.

Not only is the world as seen by quantum theorists governed by uncertainty, but it is also blessed by expressions, seeming non-sequiturs and metaphors more at home in the world of poets rather than physicists. In quantum reality, the building blocks of the universe, be they light, matter or energy, can be considered as particles – they are discrete, measurable and can travel through seemingly empty space – yet they can also be treated as waves which can interact and amplify each other, even cancel each other out. In her journals, Anaïs Nin writes that her astrologer friend Conrad Moricand understood her *modus vivendi* as being in tune with the 'larger wave lengths of my life, what he calls "*les ondes*," like some divine radio, with special antennae'.[85] In Anaïs's eyes, Moricand possessed the language of the poets when he talked of expressing the psyche in the quantum physicists' terms of oceans, waves and vibrations.

The poeticisms of quantum physics extend further: constructive interference, a wonderful occurrence between two waves, can happen when the two waves overlap and interfere with one another and the combined amplitude of the waves increases to a level greater than the individual amplitude of each wave. In this synchronising of waves, which happens when the waves form a peak or a trough at the same time even if they are on different frequencies or amplitudes, an exchange of information occurs. This can be observed with the formation of a static interference pattern that occurs when a light wave is split in two and interferes with itself. The result is a pattern of alternating black and white lines where the wave fronts are either constructively or destructively interfering with each other either to amplify or to cancel each other out.

This phenomenon is not confined to conventionally understood waves such as those of light or the ocean but, more startlingly, also defines the behaviour of the probability waves that govern the position of matter and particles such as electrons and photons. The non-intuitive notion of an electron passing through two slits at the same time with the wave probability of a half, resonating and interfering with itself to reinforce the likelihood of appearing in one place and cancelling out any likelihood of appearing in another place in a classic interference pattern has been clearly demonstrated using the famous double-slit experiments of the English scientist Thomas Young.[86]

For the scientist Karl Pribram, human beings know and experience the world in wave form by resonating with it – being in coherence with the world establishes communication with it – and the science of Herbert Frolich reveals that once fundamental particles become close enough and involved with each other enough, reaching a certain threshold of vibrating in unison and resonance, they can become 'entangled' and assume some of the more mind-boggling and non-intuitive qualities of quantum mechanics, including non-locality.

In her closing remarks on the anatomy of inspiration, the writer Rosamond Harding concludes that inspiration has much to do with a meeting of forces, or resonance. For Harding, inspiration is a result of some unknown factor accidentally meeting with an artistic or scientific mind operating and pent up with a tension caused by the accumulation of visions, colours and forms or pondering over facts in an attempt to solve a problem. The artist most capable of harnessing this emotional tension will find inspiration occurs in its highest degree within him and it will place him 'into a phase of existence different from that of his everyday world because in... the pursuit of artistic creation his own wishes and desires are overruled by his knowledge of natural sequences of events, colours, forms, rhythms, tones... he follows and *must* follow where the truth leads him.'[87] This interpretation of inspiration has elements of inevitability, resonance and contagiousness encoded in its very nature.

Modern experimental quantum physics teaches us that the passing of information between two discrete entities via vibration and coherence need not be restricted by geography. Information can be passed non-locally and instantly between two, once entangled, particles. This is a flagrant flouting of Einstein's fundamental principle that the speed of light is the upper speed limit of anything in the universe, including information, and suggests that a connection exists despite spatial distance or even temporal distance in the phase relationship between the particles.[88] Some scholars attribute the nearly simultaneous discovery of quantum mechanics itself, by Werner Heisenberg and Erwin Schrödinger, to this kind of non-local phase relationship, manifested in two scientists who were working independently of each other. Another interpretation, this time from the supernatural side, comes from *The Golden Bough*'s Sir James George Frazer who divided magic into two sympathetic types, the second being contagious magic in which two objects that were once in a relationship or in contact remain so even after they have been separated from each other. There has even been a suggestion that, if the universe was born out of the singularity that was the Big Bang, as some data would seem to suggest, then there necessarily has to be a connection between every particle in the universe. Clearly, the channelling form of inspiration as seen in the cases of George Keats and Sara Allan goes a long way to demonstrate this ethereal connection, a 'remote' kind of intervention. The critical factors in these cases of channelling include being open to the force of inspiration and having the courage to resonate and flow with its current. Rilke, who once compared himself to an anemone he had spotted in his Italian garden which was so wide open in the day that when night fell it was still as exposed, inhaling everything through its wide throat, was a devotee of this openness to resonance.[89]

One British scientist who has explored the terrain of the resonance and the non-local in terms of our memory and minds is Rupert Sheldrake, in his theory of 'morphic resonance'. In Sheldrake's theory, resonance occurs within what he calls 'morphogenetic fields'. Within these morphogenetic fields there are morphic attractors which help the morphic units to organise themselves and snap into their intended destinations within virtual chemical and biological systems, much like a ground controller guiding an aeroplane into its docking bay. The systems which the morphogenetic fields operate within will inherit habits which means that a certain permutation in a morphic field will happen with more regularity.

The inheritance of habits is critical in Sheldrake's thinking. The implication is that when nature passes a particular bit of information across generations it is dependent on neither space nor time. He uses the example of blue tits piercing the tops of the old-fashioned milk bottles which the milkman left on British doorsteps, a sight which was first spotted by ornithologists in 1921. Blue tits are a species which live for only two or so years and they do not usually travel far so, when milk delivery halted over the Second World War due to rationing, this peculiar habit, one would imagine, would have likewise halted. However, when the milkmen resumed placing the bottles on doorsteps after the war had ended, the greedy behaviour of the blue tits also resumed. Via morphic resonance and despite spatial and temporal restraint, the blue tit organism had remembered this learned behaviour. Memory may not be stored in the brain as we are used to believing but rather in a timeless type of memory bank, accessible to all across the ages. Perhaps Plato was right after all when he postulated his theory of 'anamnesis' which claimed that we all know everything there is ever to have been learnt, and that life is merely an act of remembering what we have forgotten. And lest we forget, it is the muses who, in ancient Greece, were mothered by memory herself, and who hold the key not only to our inspiration but also to the memory vaults of our time and our education in science and humanities.

Returning to the modern day, there is an inherent creativity in Sheldrake's system which is critical – that the originating pathway of the morphic unit towards its attractor is not predestined, but created by choice. Over time, morphic resonance becomes more deeply engraved as the journey towards the attractor, or the aeroplane towards its docking bay, is repeated. Like the hoof prints of animals towards the watering hole, the channel towards the attractor deepens. There was an infinite variety of ways to reach the attractor, but one route was chosen – the one with the least energy needed in order to reach it and it is at this point that a critical choice was involved. It is the creative agency which acts as a conduit for information which is important in this journey. Peculiar to muses is that they are not necessarily knowledgeable or information-laden – Lizzie Siddal did not tell Rossetti how to paint her or what to depict – but muses possess the intuitive capacity to be a catalyser of *energy* and a source of memories which is important in the role of creative agent. When Rossetti painted his Lizzie in *Beata Beatrix*, he was drawing from his associations and memories of Dante's account of the woman who has since become an archetypal figure in the arts: Beatrice.

As well as inspiration, artists employ their intuition and imagination to recognise the moment in which a ground-breaking leap has been made during their creative process, the moment when the last grain of sand sends everything tumbling into a creative chaos. Often, this leap or tumble coincides with a sense of synchronicity – of something suddenly slotting together, or of two things coinciding to create a whole much greater than the sum of its parts. It is as if an external agency has shot a thought or an idea into the mind of the artist and it is up to them, firstly to realise this concurrence and then to create something from it; the synchronicity may remain unrecognised and undeveloped in the minds of many. In order to reach this quasi-transcendental state of inspiration, the artist must give himself over to the inspiration, as Nietzsche explains: 'One hears – one does not seek; one takes – one does not ask who gives: a thought flashes out like lighting *(sic)* inevitably without hesitation – I have never had any choice about it.'[90]

Other qualities common to many great artists include a tendency to go against the status quo, patience, perseverance and the ability to live a life of synchronicity. Artists often live in the precarious path of lightning and sometimes, like Van Gogh and John Keats, risk insanity or death in the name of breaking through to a new paradigm in art. Jung had no explanation for the transmission of energy which occurs when synchronicity strikes but he went so far as to say that there were two necessary components to it, the presence of emotion coupled with an unconscious image that comes into consciousness directly or indirectly. As such, inspiration can be understood as a participatory relationship between the inspired artist and the various fields of untenable inspiration. This relationship is amplified further and catalysed more powerfully when artists are in the presence of their antennae-like muses.

Creativity and the Edge of Chaos

Common to many muses is the ability to be a lifejacket or an umbilical link for the artist in order to preserve them from the likelihood of starving, freezing or going mad. When Yoko Ono separated from John Lennon for a year and a half he was beside himself, drunk every night; Salvador Dalí almost suffocated in a diving suit when Gala wasn't with him; and, in order that Henry Miller could continue to write, Anaïs Nin sold her own typewriter and posted the profits to him.

Muses have a Janus-headed role to play in the life of the artist. Not only are they the lifelines, they can also often be on the edges themselves. Lizzie Siddal, Sylvia Plath, Joan Burroughs were all edgy, manic personality types, and Alice Liddell was perfectly positioned between childhood and adolescence when she spent that Golden Afternoon with Charles Dodgson. Many artists thrive from being near the precipices whether this be geographically, mentally or emotionally. Artists are 'outsiders' as Camus or the Angry Young Man Colin Wilson would have it and it is from these edges of humanity that they are able to glimpse new insights or make startling connections between disparate things.

In science, it is those organic systems which self-regulate which are at once the most volatile and the most creative: they are chaordic, on the tipping point of chaos and order. In a laboratory in Santa Fe a physicist called Per Bak has replicated a self-organised structure with a pile of sand. Grains are dropped slowly on to the top of the pile which, in turn, takes on a cone shape. There is a moment when the addition of one single grain of sand tips the cone's core stability over the edge and causes the entire system to collapse. The quantum physicists Ian Marshall and Danah Zohar parallel this demonstration of 'maximum responsiveness and maximum unpredictability' with the traits of adaptability and fragility found in both ecosystems and in human nature.[91] In order to be as creative as possible, Mother Nature takes evolution to the very unstable but fruitful edges for, by taking risks, novelty, in the form of new species, is born. Although traditional science struggles to deal with unpredictability, quantum science is opening up a new paradigm to deal with the nuances and turbulence associated with these unpredictable systems. It's a field which artists and muses have inhabited for millennia.

Imagine for a moment that an artist draws a single line on her canvas and is about to draw a second one. The line could become anything – from an apple to a zebra. Quantum science has revealed a startling feature of reality whereby possible futures are played out by the transition of a possibility in time. In the quantum world, the virtual transition time-travels into the future and tests out these possibilities and then, when the second line is drawn and the picture takes shape, only one of an infinite variety of images is collapsed upon. In the artistic world, it is the role of the imaginer to foresee all these possibilities and then to plump for the best possible second line – it might provoke an unexpected association, or create a completely new type of illusion or illustration: this is the genesis of genius. In science, virtual transitions may also account for the genesis of genetic development; the scientist David Bohm has compared virtual transitions to 'trial runs made in the course of nature's evolution that, though they don't themselves survive, possibly give rise to new species that do'.[92]

In the context of Leonard Shlain's belief that artists predict and foretell major transitions, there is clearly a parallel between the quantum world and that of the artists. Only those with imagination can see deeply enough to reveal startling truths or hidden similarities in differences. The writer Evelyn Underhill described this in terms of the artist being able to cross thresholds of exceptional mobility and stated that, by departing from the everyday, artists allow a latent and subliminal power to occupy their mental field. When Charles Dodgson sent Alice down the rabbit hole, he confessed it was in a bid to create a completely new field in fairy lore and yet he had no concept of what he was going to do next with his wide-eyed protagonist. It is a muse's role to energise the artist just enough to open him or her up to the infinite and sometimes crazy possibilities of what could happen next. Imagination and inspiration beat at the heart of what art and science could become.

Muses in a Participatory Universe

'Our duty, as men and women, is to proceed as if limits to our ability did not exist. We are collaborations in creation,' wrote the philosopher Pierre Teilhard de Chardin in the early twentieth century. At the beginning of the twenty-first, many of us are only just waking up to how true this aphorism rings. It is becoming increasingly apparent that relationship and context are at the heart of what we experience and know. Fritjof Capra famously explained quantum physics through the paradigm of Taoism and high-lighted the fact that subatomic particles are devoid of meaning when understood as being isolated from each other; it is only when the interconnections between them are examined that the universe begins to reveal itself. Put simply, everything is interconnected.

The role of muse can become essential during the artist's process of creating something new but only one person ever paints the canvas or writes the manuscript or musical score. Yet the legendary John Lennon and WB Yeats both attributed their greatest successes to a collaboration of some sort with their muses. Lennon said that Yoko Ono was his Don Juan, who taught him everything he knew and inspired all creativity in him. George Yeats's role in composing *A Vision* was fundamental to its very creation, which WB Yeats realised. Remember it was he who said that no mind's contents are necessarily shut off from another's. Muses help to bring the world into being through channelling the inspiration, like a divine gift.

Due to the infinite and indeterminate possibilities of the quantum nature of reality, it is the case that everything is mutually possible until a wave function collapses and reality reveals itself – this collapse is not down to some scientific equation, but down to the observer taking notice of the world. Frustratingly, this 'observer' cannot be located anywhere in the human anatomy. It remains a mystery as to what it actually *is* which observes but it is understood that, by virtue of a mutual exchange of being observed and being the observer, the world comes into existence. The concrete world and the observer are not discrete; there is no distinction between subject and object, inner and outer, or this and that in the quantum world. Just as Lindsay Clarke describes how, in the powerful moment of feeling inspired, the artist can revel in his connection to a world soul, for quantum scientists this universe is similarly participatory and is one in which consciousness has a leading role to play in co-creating reality.

The British lutenist Anthony Rooley has examined the role of the observer and the performer on stage in his book *Performance: Revealing the Orpheus Within*. In his schema, the performer is not the creator of the performance, rather he is 'responding to and transmitting a force of creative energy and inspiration which is not of their making'. By performing (literally 'to bring into form') in front of the observer the performer brings into being powers, energy and inspiration which were latent on the un-formed stage. The role of the artist performing is one of a 'porter, a carrier, a transmitter, dipping into the subtle non-formed world and manifesting it in the tangible world of form'.[93] Rooley believes that the great performers are like messengers – they communicate and channel a creative inspiration. In the paradigm of quantum physics and Zero Point Field theory, scientists would say that the performer is getting on the same wavelength, reaching out into the future to bring an interpretation to the stage.

Rainer Maria Rilke was at home on the edges of humanhood and understood what it meant to fully give oneself over to inspiration in order to create. He believed that there was neither a here nor a beyond, rather that there was a 'great unity in which the beings that surpass us, the 'angels', are at home… We of the here and now are not for a moment hedged in the time-world, nor confined within it… we are incessantly flowing over and over to those who preceded us.'[94] Not only are people free from the constraints of time and space, if Rilke and quantum physics are to be believed, but people are also at liberty to exercise their imaginations and make these mind-images real. A dangerous idea ethically, but in practice this is how art happens. It is hard for us to imagine both possibilities of a cat, to take Erwin Schrödinger's example, being both alive and dead, or that the nature of a fundamental entity, be it a photon of light or an atom's electron, is necessarily defined and manifested by the observer.

The quantum world is magically unpredictable and marvellously undetermined: what better conditions for muses to flex their inspirational muscles in the lives of great artists? Quantum physics opens up the imagination to a plethora of possibilities where the possibility of mutually contradictory ways of observing something at the same time becomes a reality. When muses are in synch with their artists, they perform a very special role in the dance of creativity to reveal the nature of inspiration afresh each time. But even to discriminate between muse and artist does a disservice to inspiration, for ultimately there is no division between Van Gogh and Gauguin, or Yeats and his psychic wife. To create a work of art is to create a relationship with something beyond one's ego or one's immediate reality, and to be a muse is to plug into that powerful, divine, universal, oceanic and invisible energy which surrounds each and every one of us.

End Notes

[1] GM Hopkins, from a letter to Baillie, 10 September 1864 published in *Further Letters of Gerard Manley Hopkins* Claude Colleer Abbott (editor), Oxford University Press, 1956.

[2] Quoted in *My Yorkshire Life* magazine, July 2001, p.129.

[3] Robert Graves, *The White Goddess*, Carcanet, 1997, p.438.

[4] The man draped across the sofa isn't Salvador Dalí himself, but the lead actor Lorenzo Quinn from the 1991 biopic, *Dalí*.

[5] Pausanias, *Guide to Ancient Greece, Vol. 1: Central Greece Book IX*, Peter Levi (editor), Penguin, 1971, p.368.

[6] Hesiod, *Theogony*, ML West (translator), Oxford University Press, 1988, lines 1–3.

[7] Hesiod, lines 27–8.

[8] Graves, p.20.

[9] Plato, *Phaedrus and Letters VII and VIII*, Walter Hamilton (translator), Penguin, 1973, line 245.

[10] Plato, *Ion* in *The Collected Dialogues*, Edith Hamilton and Huntington Cairns (editors), Bollingen Series LXXI, Princeton University Press, 1989, line 534e.

[11] Cited in Jerry Brotton, *The Renaissance Bazaar: From Silk Road to Michelangelo*, Oxford University Press, 2002, p.22.

[12] Cited in Brotton, p.20.

[13] Reproduced in *The Letters of Marsilio Ficino,* Language Department of the School of Economic Science, London (translators), Shepheard Walwyn, 1975.

[14] Cited in *The Troubadours: An Introduction,* Simon Gaunt and Sarah Kay (editors), Cambridge University Press, 1999, p.1.

[15] Epigraph quoted in the opening pages to Meg Bogin, *The Women Troubadours,* WW Norton and Company, 1980.

[16] *How Poets Work*, Tony Curtis (editor), Seren, 1996, pp.165–66.

[17] Curtis, pp.165–66.

[18] Quoted from the Introduction to Yeats, *A Vision,* in Ann Saddlemyer, *Becoming George: The Life of Mrs WB Yeats*, Oxford University Press, 2002, p.103.

[19] Quoted from Alexander Norman Jeffares, *WB Yeats: Man and Poet,* in Saddlemyer, p.127.

[20] Quoted from a letter written 31 October 1818 in Joanna Richardson, *Fanny Brawne: A Biography,* Thames & Hudson, 1952, p.20.

[21] Richardson, p.22.

[22] Richardson, p.36.

[23] Letter dated October 1819.

[24] Letter to George and Thomas Keats dated 21 December 1817.

[25] Graves, p.440.

[26] Diane Middlebrook, *Her Husband: Hughes and Plath – A Marriage,* Little, Brown, 2004, p.xv.

[27] Account of Ted and Sylvia's meeting can be found on

pp.210–12 in Sylvia Plath, *The Journals of Sylvia Plath 1950–1962,* Karen V. Kukil (editor), Faber and Faber, 2002.

[28] Quoted in Middlebrook, p.xvi and excerpted from an interview for the BBC *Two of A Kind,* January 1961.

[29] Middlebrook, p.226.

[30] Quoted in Erica Wagner, *Ariel's Gift: Ted Hughes, Sylvia Plath and the Story of Birthday Letters,* Faber and Faber, 2000, p.5.

[31] David Sheff, *Last Interview: All We Are Saying – John Lennon and Yoko Ono Interviews,* G. Barry Golson (editor), Sidgwick & Jackson, 2000, p.187.

[32] Jann S. Wenner, *Lennon Remembers: The Full Rolling Stone Interviews from 1970,* Verso, 2000, p.106.

[33] Wenner, p.151.

[34] Tim McGirk, *Wicked Lady: Salvador Dali's Muse,* Hutchinson, 1989, p.160.

[35] McGirk, p.10.

[36] Quoted in Francine Prose, *The Lives of the Muses: Nine Women and the Artists They Inspired*, Aurum, 2004, p.211.

[37] Anaïs Nin, *The Journals of Anaïs Nin, Volume Two,* Quartet Books, 1974, p.196.

[38] Henry Miller, *Letters to Anaïs Nin*, Gunther Stuhlmann (editor), Peter Owen, 1965, p.13.

[39] Miller to Nin from Lycée Carnot, Dijon, 4 February 1932.

[40] Nin, p.97.

[41] Nin, p.265.

[42] Nin, p.215.

[43] Quoted in Martin Gayford, *The Yellow House: Van Gogh, Gauguin and Nine Turbulent Weeks in Arles,* Penguin, 2006. Gayford's book is the most recent to explore the ill-fated mutual musedom relationship.

[44] *The Letters of Vincent van Gogh to his Brother and Others, 1872–1890,* with a memoir by his sister-in-law Joanna van Gogh-Bonger (abridger Elfreda Powell), Constable, 2003, p.ii.

[45] Quoted in Gayford, p.183.

[46] *Dear Theo: An Autobiography of Vincent Van Gogh from His Letters,* Irving Stone (editor), Constable and Company, 1937, p.468.

[47] Vincent Van Gogh, *The Letters of Vincent Van Gogh*, Ronald de Leeuw (editor), Arnold Pomerans (translator), Allen Lane, The Penguin Press, 1996, p.422.

[48] Gayford, p.321.

[49] Richard Holmes, *Coleridge: Early Visions,* Flamingo, 1999, p.99n.

[50] Quoted from Wordsworth's *Memoirs* quoted in Rosamond EM Harding, *Anatomy of Inspiration,* W Heffer & Sons, 1948, p.31.

[51] Samuel Taylor Coleridge, *Biographia Literaria*, The Everyman Library, 1977, chapter 14, pp.184–5.

[52] William Wordsworth and ST Coleridge, *Lyrical Ballads,* 1798 Edition, Oxford University Press, 1979, p.173.

[53] Coleridge also contributed *The Foster-Mother's Tale, The Nightingale, a Conversational Poem* and *The Dungeon*.

[54] Samuel Taylor Coleridge, *Biographia Literaria Vol. I,* Bollingen Series, James Engell and W. Jackson Bate

(editors), Princeton University Press and Routledge, 1987, p.12.

[55] Edited by Rosalie Mander, Dalrymple Press, 1984.

[56] Quoted in *Conversations with William S. Burroughs*, Peggy Whitman Prenshaw (editor), University Press of Mississippi, 1999, p.211.

[57] www.bbc.co.uk/bbcfour/audiointerviews/profilepages/burroughsw1.shtml

[58] Letter written in Lebensrückblick and quoted in Lou Andreas-Salomé, *You Alone Are Real to Me*, Angela von der Lippe (translator), BOA Editions, 2003, p.139.

[59] In *My Sister, My Spouse*, Victor Gollancz, 1963.

[60] Peters, p.215.

[61] Cited in Prose, p.183.

[62] Peters, p.210.

[63] Written from Duino bei Nabresina, 10 January 1912.

[64] Rilke to Lou from Oberneuland bei Bremen, 8 August 1903.

[65] Salomé, p.105.

[66] Rilke to Lou from Paris, 26 June 1914.

[67] Salomé, p.139.

[68] Salomé, p.127.

[69] The playwright Mark Burgess has adapted the story of the inspiration behind *Chitty Chitty Bang Bang* for the radio in his play *From Father With Love*, Pier Production, 2006.

[70] In *Lucia Joyce: To Dance in the Wake*, Farrar, Straus & Giroux, 2003.

[71] Lewis Carroll, *Alice on the Stage*, in *The Theatre*, 1 April 1887, vol. IX New Series, pp.210–11.

[72] Letter dated 10 June, 1864, as cited in *Aspects of Alice,* Robert Phillips (editor), Penguin, 1971.

[73] Carroll, pp.179–184.

[74] In *Poetry and the Age,* Faber and Faber, 1955.

[75] Dated 12 March 2006.

[76] Interview conducted by the author with Lindsay Clarke in August 2006.

[77] Ken Wilber, *Theory of Everything,* Gateway, 2001, p.267.

[78] Theodore Zeldin, *An Intimate History of Humanity,* Random House, 1998, pp.160–61.

[79] *The Creative Process: A Revealing Study of Genius At Work,* Brewster Ghiselin (editor), Mentor, 1952, p.58.

[80] Quoted in Morton D Paley, *Energy and the Imagination: A Study of the Development of Blake's Thought,* Clarendon Press, 1970, p.2.

[81] CG Jung, *Memories, Dreams, Reflections,* Fontana Press, 1995, pp.234–35.

[82] Zero Point Field has been given a thorough overview in Lynne McTaggart, *The Field: The Quest for the Secret Force of the Universe,* HarperCollins, 2003.

[83] Zeldin, p.466.

[84] McTaggart, p.125.

[85] Nin, p.116.

[86] Brian Green, *The Fabric of the Cosmos,* Penguin, 2004 pp.85–88.

[87] Harding, p.111.

[88] McTaggart, pp.108–9 and p.63.

[89] Salomé, in a letter from Rilke written in Paris on 26 June 1914, p.80.

[90] Ghiselin, pp.202–203.

[91] Ian Marshall and Danah Zohar, *Who's Afraid of Schrödinger's Cat? The New Science Revealed: Quantum Theory, Relativity, Chaos and the New Cosmology,* Bloomsbury, 1997, p.134.

[92] Marshall and Zohar, pp.374–75.

[93] Anthony Rooley, *Performance: Revealing The Orpheus Within,* Element, 1990, p.25.

[94] Rainer Maria Rilke, *Letters of Rainer Maria Rilke, 1910–1924,* Jane Barnard Green and MM Herter (translators), Norton, 1947, pp.373–74.

Selected Bibliography

Allison, John, *A Way of Seeing: Perception, Imagination and Poetry*, Herndon, Virginia: Lindisfarne Books, 2003

Bancroft, Randy, *Schrödinger's Cat & The Golden Bough: Reflections on Science, Mythology and Magic,* Lanham, Maryland. University Press of America, 2000

Baring, Ann and Cashford, Jules, *The Myth of the Goddess: Evolution of an Image*, London: Viking, 1991

Bate, Walter Jackson, *Negative Capability: An Intuitive Approach in Keats*, Cambridge, Massachusetts: Harvard University Press, 1939

Bogin, Meg, *The Women Troubadours*, New York: WW Norton and Company, 1980

Brotton, Jerry, *The Renaissance Bazaar: From Silk Road to Michelangelo*, Oxford: Oxford University Press, 2002

Burroughs, William, *Letters of William Burroughs 1945–1949,* Oliver Harris (editor), London: Picador, 1993

Capra, Fritjof, *The Tao of Physics*, London: Flamingo, 1992

Capra, Fritjof, *Buddhist Physics,* Schumacher UK Bristol Lectures, October 1979

Carroll, Lewis, *Alice in Wonderland,* Lisbeth Zwerger (illustrator), New York: North-South Books, 1999

Carroll, Lewis *Alice on the Stage* in *The Theatre,* Vol. IX, New Series, 1 April 1887

Clark, Anne, *The Real Alice*, London: Michael Joseph, 1981

Clarke, Lindsay, *Imagining Otherwise,* GreenSpirit Pamphlet No. 6, 2004

Coleridge, Samuel Taylor, *Biographia Literaria*, London: The Everyman Library, 1997

Curtis, Tony (editor), *How Poets Work*, Bridgend: Seren, 1996

Dante, Alighieri, *The New Life* Dante Gabriel Rossetti (translator), New York: New York Review Books, 2002

Dante, Alighieri, *The Divine Comedy* Vols 1 and 2, Robert M. Durling (translator), Ronald L. Martinez (editor), Oxford: Oxford University Press, 2002 and 2003

Dunn, Henry Treffry, *Recollections of Dante Gabriel Rossetti and His Circle,* Rosalie Mander (editor), London: Dalrymple Press, 1984

Ficino, Marsilio, *The Letters of Marsilio Ficino* Vol. 1, Language Department of the School of Economic Science, London (translators), London: Shepheard Walwyn, 1975

Fideler, David (editor), *Reviving the Academies of The Muses* in *Alexandria 3: Cosmology, Philosophy, Myth and Culture*, York Beach, Maine: Phanes Press, 1995

Gaunt, Simon and Kay, Sarah (editors), *The Troubadours: An Introduction*, Cambridge: Cambridge University Press, 1999

Gayford, Martin, *The Yellow House: Van Gogh, Gauguin and*

Nine Turbulent Weeks in Arles, London: Penguin, 2006

Ghiselin, Brewster (editor), *The Creative Process: A Revealing Study of Genius At Work,* New York: Mentor, 1952

Graves, Robert, *The White Goddess*, Manchester: Carcanet Press, 1997

Graves, Robert, *The Greek Myths,* Michel W Pharand (editor), Manchester: Carcanet Press, 2001

Habicht, Christian, *Pausanias' Guide to Ancient Greece*, Berkeley: University of California Press, 1985

Harding, Rosamond EM, *An Anatomy of Inspiration*, Cambridge: W Heffer & Sons, 1948

Harper, George Mills, *The Making of Yeats's A Vision* Vol. 1, London: Macmillan, 1987

Hawksley, Lucinda, *Lizzie Siddal: The Tragedy of a Pre-Raphelite Supermodel*, London: André Deutsch, 2005

Hendry, JF, *The Sacred Threshold: A Life of Rainer Maria Rilke*, Manchester: Carcanet Press, 1983

Hesiod, *Theogony,* ML West (translator), Oxford: Oxford University Press, 1988

Holmes, Richard, *Coleridge: Early Visions,* London: Flamingo, 1999

Jung, CG, *Memories, Dreams, Reflections*, Richard and Clara Winston (translators), London: Fontana Press, 1995

Jung, CG, *Aspects of the Feminine,* RFC Hull (translator), London: Routledge, 1982

Jung, CG, *Synchronicity: An Acausal Connecting Principle,* RFC Hull (translator), Bollingen Series, Princeton: Princeton University Press, 1973

Kaufman James C, and Baer, John (editors), *Creativity Across*

Domains: Faces of the Muse, New Jersey: Lawrence Erlbaum Associates, 2005

King, Karen L, *What is Gnosticism?*, Cambridge, Massachussetts: Harvard University Press, 2003

Laszlo, Ervin, *Science and the Re-Enchantment of the World*, audio recording by the Scientific and Medical Network, SM146, London, June 2006

Lovett, Charles C, *Alice on Stage*, Meckler, 1990

Marsh, Jan, *The Legend of Elizabeth Siddal*, London: Quartet Books, 1989

Marshall, Ian and Zohar, Danah, *Who's Afraid of Schrödinger's Cat? The New Science Revealed: Quantum Theory, Relativity, Chaos and the New Cosmology*, London: Bloomsbury, 1997

McGirk, Tim, *Wicked Lady: Salvador Dali's Muse*, London: Hutchinson, 1989

McTaggart, Lynne, *The Field: The Quest for the Secret Force of the Universe*, London: HarperCollins, 2003

Middlebrook, Diane, *Her Husband: Hughes and Plath — A Marriage*, London: Little, Brown, 2004

Miller, Henry, *Letters to Anaïs Nin,* Gunther Stuhlmann (editor), London: Peter Owen, 1965

Murray, Penelope and Wilson, Peter (editors), *Music and the Muses: The Culture of 'Mousike' in the Classical Athenian City*, Oxford: Oxford University Press, 2004

Nancy, Jean-Luc, *The Muses*, Palo Alto, California: Stanford University Press, 1996

Nemeczek, Alfred, *Van Gogh in Arles*, London: Prestel, 1995

Nin, Anaïs, *The Journals of Anaïs Nin, Volume Two*, London: Quartet Books, 1974

Paley, Morton D, *Energy and the Imagination: A Study of the Development of Blake's Thought*, Oxford: Clarendon Press, 1970

Pausanias, *Guide to Greece Vol. 1: Central Greece Book IX,* Peter Levi (editor), London: Penguin, 1971

Peters, Heinz Frederick, *My Sister My Spouse,* London: Victor Gollancz, 1963

Phillips, Adam, *My Inspiration, Observer*, Review, 12 March 2006

Phillips, Robert (editor), *Aspects of Alice*, London: Penguin, 1971

Plath, Sylvia, *The Journals of Sylvia Plath 1950–1962,* Karen V. Kukil (editor), London: Faber and Faber, 2000

Plato, *The Collected Dialogues,* Edith Hamilton and Huntington Cairns (editors) Bollingen Series LXXI, Princeton: Princeton University Press, 1989

Plato, *Phaedrus and Letters VII and VIII,* Walter Hamilton (translator), London: Penguin, 1973

Prenshaw, Peggy Whitman (general editor), *Conversations with William S. Burroughs*, Jackson, Mississippi: University Press of Mississippi, 1999

Prose, Francine, *The Lives of the Muses: Nine Women and the Artists They Inspired*, London: Aurum Press, 2004

Richardson, Joanna, *Fanny Brawne: A Biography*, London: Thames & Hudson, 1952

Rilke, Rainer Maria, *Selected Letters 1902–1926*, London: Quartet Books, 1988

Rilke, Rainer Maria, *Letters of Rainer Maria Rilke 1910–1924,* Jane Barnard Green and MM Herter (translators), New York: WW Norton, 1947

Rooley, Anthony, *Performance: Revealing The Orpheus Within*, Shaftesbury: Element, 1990

Rothenberg, Albert, *Creativity and Madness*, Baltimore: Johns Hopkins University Press, 1990

Runco, Mark A & Pritzker, Steven R (editors), *Encyclopedia of Creativity Vols 1 and 2*, Academic Press, 1999

Saddlemyer, Ann, *Becoming George: The Life of Mrs WB Yeats*, Oxford: Oxford University Press, 2002

Salomé, Lou Andreas, *You Alone Are Real to Me*, Angela von der Lippe (translator), Rochester, New York: BOA Editions, 2003

Salomé, Lou Andreas, *Looking Back: Memoirs by Lou Andreas Salomé,* Ernst Pfeiffer (editor), Breon Mitchell (translator), Paragon House, 1991

Schmidt, Michael, *Lives of the Poets*, London: Phoenix, 1998

Sheff, David, *Last Interview: All We Are Saying — John Lennon and Yoko Ono Interviews,* G. Barry Golson (editor), London: Sidgwick & Jackson, 2000

Sheldrake, Rupert, *A New Science of Life: The Hypothesis of Formative Causation*, London: Anthony Blond, 1981

Sheldrake, Rupert, *The Sense of Being Stared At*, London: Hutchinson, 2003

Shlain, Leonard, *Art and Physics*, New York: William Morrow, 1991

Shloss, Carol Loeb, *Lucia Joyce: To Dance in the Wake*, New York: Farrar, Straus & Giroux, 2003

Spentzou, Efrossini and Fowler, Don (editors), *Cultivating The Muse: Struggles for Power and Inspiration in Classical*

Literature, Oxford: Oxford University Press, 2002

Stone, Irving (editor), *Dear Theo: An Autobiography of Vincent Van Gogh from His Letters*, London: Constable and Company, 1937

Storr, Anthony, *The Dynamics of Creation*, London: Secker & Warburg, 1972

Thalbourne, Michael A, *Transliminality and Creativity*, pp.193–202 *Journal of Creative Behaviour* Vol. 34, No. 3, Third Quarter, 2000

Van Gogh, Vincent, *The Letters of Vincent Van Gogh*, Ronald de Leeuw (editor), Arnold Pomerans (translator), London: Allen Lane, 1996

Van Gogh, Vincent, *The Letters of Vincent van Gogh to his Brother and Others, 1872–1890* with a memoir by his sister-in-law Joanna van Gogh-Bonger (abridger Elfreda Powell), London: Constable, 2003

Wagner, Erica, *Ariel's Gift: Ted Hughes, Sylvia Plath and the Story of Birthday Letters*, London: Faber and Faber, 2000

Walker, Benjamin, *Encyclopaedia of Esoteric Man*, London: Routledge and Kegan Paul, 1977

Wenner, Jann S, *Lennon Remembers: The Full Rolling Stone Interviews from 1970*, London: Verso, 2000

Wilber, Ken, *A Theory of Everything*, Gateway, 2001

Wordsworth, William and Coleridge, ST, *Lyrical Ballads 1798*, second edition, WJB Owen (editor), Oxford: Oxford University Press, 1979

Yates, Frances, *The Art of Memory*, London: Pimlico, 1992

Yeats, WB, *The Collected Works of WB Yeats, Vol. 1: The Poems (Revised)*, Richard J. Finneran (editor), London:

Macmillan, 1983

Yeats, WB, *If I Were Four-and-Twenty*, Dundrum: The Cuala Press, 1940

Yeats, WB, *A Vision,* Second edition, London: Macmillan, 1962

Zeldin, Theodore, *An Intimate History of Humanity*, London: Random House, 1998

Zohar, Dana, *The Quantum Self*, London: Flamingo, 1990

Index

INDEX

Primitive Mythology, 22
psychology, 26, 39, 123
Pythagoras, 22, 28

relationships, 16, 34–35, 47, 54,
    57–58, 61, 63–66, 68–69, 76,
    83, 86–87, 98–99, 103,
    107–108, 120, 128, 132, 135
resonance, 27, 112, 127–130
Rilke, Rainer Maria, 87, 95–101,
    129, 137–138
Rime of the Ancient Mariner, The,
    82
Rodin, Auguste, 98
Rooley, Anthony, 137
Rossetti, Dante Gabriel, 85–91,
    94, 131

Salomé, Lou Andreas, 87, 95
Schopenhauer, Arthur, 13
Schrödinger, Erwin, 128, 138
science, 16, 21–22, 119–120, 123,
    125, 127, 130, 133–135
Sheldrake, Rupert, 129–130
Shlain, Leonard, 120–121, 135
Siddal, Lizzie, 85, 89, 115, 131,
    133
Socrates, 23–25
soul, the, 15, 24–25, 27–28,
    34–35, 39, 61, 79, 94, 112,
    137
Stone, Irving, 75
supernatural, 43, 81–82, 128

Tchaikovsky, 13
Theogony, 20
Thomas, 42
Tropic of Cancer, 67–68
Tropic of Capricorn, 67
troubadours, 31–33

Underhill, Evelyn, 135
universe, the, 28, 67, 120, 123,
    125, 128–129, 136–137

Van Gogh, Vincent, 73–78, 83,
    132, 138
West, Mae, 15
Wevill, Assia, 56–57
White Goddess, The, 19, 51
Wilber, Ken, 113
Wordsworth, Dorothy, 79
Wordsworth, William, 73, 78–83
writing, 23, 31–33, 40, 44, 46–48,
    52, 55–57, 60, 68–70, 81–82,
    98–99, 101, 104, 116

Yeats, Bertha George, 39–44,
    115–116, 136
Yeats, William Butler, 39–44, 136,
    138

Zeldin, Theodore, 111, 113–115,
    123
Zero Point Field, 123–124
Zeus, 21